AND SATURDAY IS CHRISTMAS

AND SATURDAY IS CHRISTMAS:
New and Selected Poems

Maurice Rutherford

*For Mary –
on your Birthday –
with love,*

Maurice

Shoestring Press

x x x

9th September 2015

Printed by imprintdigital
Upton Pyne, Exeter
www.imprintdigital.net

Typeset by Nathanael Ravenlock
nat@ravenlock.eu

Published by Shoestring Press
19 Devonshire Avenue, Beeston, Nottingham, NG9 1BS
(0115) 925 1827
www.shoestringpress.co.uk

First published 2011
© Copyright: Maurice Rutherford
The moral right of the author has been asserted.
ISBN 978 1 907356 21 6

'Ah, fill the cup:- what boots it to repeat
How Time is slipping underneath our feet:
Unborn tomorrow, and dead yesterday,
Why fret about them if today be sweet!'

Edward Fitzgerald
(From *The Rubaiyat of Omar Khayyam*)

Olive — for the good times

ACKNOWLEDGEMENTS

The Selected Poems are taken from Maurice Rutherford's three published books, *Slipping The Tugs* (Lincolnshire and Humberside Arts, 1982), *This Day Dawning* (Peterloo Poets, 1989), *Love Is A Four-Letter World* (Peterloo Poets, 1994) and one pamphlet *After the Parade* (Shoestring Press, 1996).

Of the New Poems 'Counting the Cards' was first published in *Speaking English*, ed. Andy Croft (Five Leaves Press, 2007). 'Role-play' and 'QED' appear in the Philip Larkin Society Journal *About Larkin,* ed. Janet Brennan and James Booth. With the exception of twelve poems published by Eyelet Books in 2010 under the title *Funny Old World* the remaining poems are previously unpublished.

Contents

Introduction   i

SLIPPING THE TUGS

Poem on Saturday   3
The Cycle   4
The Other Grandad   5
The Quiet Men   6
Heinz Gropsmeyer   7
Painting in Port   8
Ship's Husband   9
Strikebound   10
Welsh Estuary   11
Cuckoo   12
To My Wife…   13
Solatium   14
Sonnet: Through Mother's Eyes   15

THIS DAY DAWNING

Effects   19
Intake   20
Interlude   22
A Chat with Susan   23
Assignation   26
Timekeeper   26
Fitter   27
Bilge-Diver   28
Canteen Assistant   29
Old Book-Keeper   30
The Bottle Bank   32
Outlook on Monday   33

Pied Wagtails   34
Magazines in a Waiting-Room   35
Duchess   36
Neighbours   37
Curriculum Vitae   38
The Sting   40
Words   41
Epithalamium   43
All You Need is Love   44
Bacalao   46
Anniversary   47
The Gazebo   48
This Day Dawning   49
Love Story   51

LOVE IS A FOUR-LETTER WORLD

The Light of the World   55
Peter's House   56
Tutorial   58
The Cod Farm   59
Solitaire   60
Woman in the Crowd   61
In Vacuo   62
Love of an Autumn Afternoon   63
Mrs. Cholmondeley   63
Comforts   65
Lessons in Age   66
Solstice   68
Remnants   69
Pillow-Talk   70
Autumn Lodge — The Dayroom   71
Ex Libris   72
O Tempora! O Mores!   73
A View of the Sea   74

Moment in History   75
Skulls at Phnom Penh   76
Once More, On War   77
All Down the Avenue   80
Half-Term   81
Only Connect   82
The Hull Poets – And Pigeons   83
Lime Street to Paragon   85
On Saving the Non-Winners Pile for
Re-Use as Draft-Paper   86
The Reading   87
Dear Mr. George   89
Bolt for Freedom   91
Recapture   92
Mr Larkin   94
This Be the Curse   95
Rome is so Bad   96
The Autumn Outings   96
Postscript to My Father   99

AFTER THE PARADE

A High Horizon, 1927   103
Being There   103
An Ideal Couple   104
The Bit-Bag   104
Flu Survivor   105
That's Channel 4 News   106
Her Green   107
Rothbury Revisited   108
Carrot Cake   108
Gilfillan   109
Ulysses Smith   109
Brewer   110
House Guest   111

View from Hessle Road 112
Over the Rainbow 112
Displaced Persons 113
After the Parade… 114

AND SATURDAY IS CHRISTMAS

A Tree in St. Andrew's 117
Santos to Santa Cruz Della Sierra 125
A Novice Stacker Talks Herself to Sleep 126
Funny Old World 127
The World at Eight 128
The World at Twelve 129
A Wind Getting Up 130
Kinderwelt 131
Mist 131
Short Straw 132
Pre-Op 133
The Music-Man 134
Lady of the Town 135
A Poetry Anorak Recalls Some House Guests 135
Turkey and Tinsel 137
Counting the Cards 137
Driftwood 138
On His Silence 140
Roots 141
Behind the Lines 142
Domestic Science 144
Leylandiisaurus Radix 145
Red Admiral 146
English and the F-Word 147
Gloss on Three Guests 148
Rosie 151

Birth of a Great-Granddaughter, 15.11.2009   152
Parliament Website, 18.06.2009   153
Upon Westminster Bridge   154
Nosejob   155
Role-Play   158
QED   159
Letter to Edith Södergran   160
Forlimpópoli   161
La Gioiosa Et Amorosa
Pinot Grigio Blush   162
Innocence, 1960   163
Experience, 2010   164
Time   165
Lights Out   166
The Fertile Year   167
Look, Twice   168
After Our Diamond   168
Light   169
Going Off Piste   170

NOTES

INTRODUCTION

As he tells us in his fine, angry elegy for the poet-composer Ivor Gurney, Maurice Rutherford was born "the same day that they locked away/ the music-man insane." ("The Music-Man"). 1922 was the birth-year of another poet who fires Rutherford's imagination, that eventual Hull-resident, Philip Larkin. The two never met in person, but it was Larkin's Oxford anthology that Rutherford chose as his guide when, after a long career as a ship-repairer's technical writer, he began his ascent of the Mount Purgatory of twentieth-century English poetry.

Manual work, like poetry-making, is a significant theme for Rutherford. An early poem, "Ship's Husband," presents vivid, sinewy portraits of an old seaman "pushing his bow-wave against the brunt/ of years" and his ever-vigorous wife with her "pumice face,/ her busy arms conger-strong and firm." Rutherford's characters often refuse to be defined by their jobs: there's the "Fitter" ("You've never seen the badger's bum/ he's reputedly as rough as") transformed to "Rambler, angler, wildfowler when he's free" and the "Bilge-Diver" with "his shift-long repertoire" of Frank Sinatra hits. It's not that these portraits are colourful, though they are, but that, like all Rutherford's observations, they are authentic. The narratives derive from an intimate understanding of working lives, the physical demands of the different trades, and the psychological accommodations.

The matter of class inequalities is addressed in a later poem, "The Autumn Outings." Here, in a spirit of rebellion and admiration, Rutherford revises "The Whitsun Weddings," taking the same complex stanza that Larkin devised, but the view-point of a manager of a small company forced into liquidation - an ordinary,

i

decent man who, on a happier day, might have been among the wedding-guests in Larkin's poem. It is a hard-hitting tour-de-force.

Rutherford is a master of his craft, whether celebrating the "Birth of a Great Grand-Daughter" in his favourite set-form, the sonnet, or exploring a less-familiar poetic import, the glose, in a "Gloss on Three Guests," where he entwines new-shaped poems around lines from Frances Horovitz, Yevtushenko and R. S. Thomas. He is a deft coiner of words and phrases (*upmanship, go-go area for dogs, workthrift years, drowse-by date*), dipping into the lexicons of other languages where appropriate. He can securely wire a whole poem with a single powerful metaphor, as in "Anniversary," or give the reader a small, pleasant electric-shock by means of the unusual poetic technique known as codology.

And Saturday is Christmas ranges through war-poems, political poems, elegies, love poems, travelogues and wry meditations on aging. The mind operating in all these fields is open, engaged, fond of the human species, though sometimes angry and always passionately interested in social justice. A writer's age, whether 18 or 80, should not automatically qualify him or her for admiration, but the poet who, with the necessary skills and talent, can draw on decades of varied experiences, and chronicle them with compassion, humour and meticulous truthfulness, demands our full attention. Maurice Rutherford is that poet.

Carol Rumens, 2011

SLIPPING THE TUGS

POEM ON SATURDAY

Outside my window, a linnet on the laburnum
shows poetry to the other birds, preens,
stutters its wings and corrugates away
across the lawn, and the nest of words
I am waiting to hatch goes cold.

Yesterday, as from the office window I watched
a vessel leave the lockpits, outward bound
for Genoa, slipping the tugs from the task in hand
my feet were treading Italian ground
before the Humber had healed in her wake.

I knew, once, a tall school window high above
the tiers of desks where, in carbolic air,
peas imprisoned in a jar strove for the sky
and begged me join in their climb to the place where
every day is Saturday and Saturday is Christmas.

THE CYCLE

I was tall enough then to stand on the lower pedal
of his cycle leaned against the veranda front
and see my face, moon-stretched, in the bell
in whose forbidden ring I heard names of magic places
beyond the garden gate—Bowlalley Lane, Springhead,
Little Switzerland, Land of Green Ginger and Wincolmlee.

Sometimes I'd be allowed to meet him, just beyond
the passage-end, returning home from work, and then
he'd crook me in his arm up onto the saddle
and carry my pride high on the cycle home. I remember
the thrill of that, my impatience for the dangling legs
to grow, and the sure salt-cod smell from his coat sleeve
favouring me against the danger of a fall.

Sometimes, when he let me take his newspapers
from the saddlebag, there were sandwiches
left from lunch—made for him the previous night—
now crisped and curled at the corners,
and I'd enjoy, almost, the taste of adult fare
through a mustard-tortured tongue.

A generation later, crooking my arm and easing him
into the car, I saw anticipation light his face,
starting on a journey to countryside or shore
where we would sit and savour sandwiches and talk
of White City, Swanland, Rotenhering Staithe,
Sammy's Point and Argyle Street bridge, Gloucester Street.

THE OTHER GRANDAD

It is the waistcoat I remember most,
and the walking-stick to ease the weight
from slow feet in bloated boots; a parcel
of dark red steak in the yellowed paper
of its day and gift-wrapped in a newspaper.
"Fry it for me Maud, will you?"
He shouldn't have come, I knew;
he wasn't very clean, relieved himself
at the backyard sink, and made
unpardonable noises without "Pardon."

Once, arriving taxied at the City Hall
fancy-dressed for the Mayoress's Ball,
we saw him propping the pillars, with his kind.
We didn't greet, but passed and went inside,
then Dad slipped out again to shake his hand
with a cold half-crown.

I don't remember his face,
just a brown waistcoat, black-bright
between buttons; and the fat, splashed boots.

THE QUIET MEN

They boast, of deeds performed the night before,
of conquests in dark alleys of their minds,
of gallons drunk and women satisfied,
erecting pedestals and laying claims
on which to build their reputations high
in up-manship and camaraderie.

By day they learn the drills and skills of war,
defile dead ground, find trees with bushy tops
as aids to indication; march at ease,
sing ribaldry and urinate the lanes,
but never ask the question burning deep
beyond the chilling sweat, preceding sleep.

These were the quiet men before they came–
from homes like yours and mine one may suppose,
and on this battle-eve some say their prayers,
and most are virgins if the truth be told;
tomorrow there'll be taller tales to tell
and quieter men for telling them as well.

HEINZ GROPSMEYER

Almost forty years and your name still moves,
shrapnel under the skin, on reflective days.
You were not much older then than in the *Wehrmacht*
photograph above your name, twenty to my twentytwo.
Your canvas pack told more of you – *Kölnischwasser,*
talcum, *Rotbart* blades – though you had not lain
long enough to grow death's beard. More the lad
down someone's street than hated Hun or Boche
the jackboots made of you.

I tried to pull off the boots, not to ease
your stiff feet but perhaps to please mine
or strip the camouflage from common fundamentals.
I had heard, in school, of your brown shirt,
summer camp and sung-devotion to the Fatherland;
in your new fieldgrey, singing your *Horst Wessel* song
could you have known that we, too, paraded colours
into church for blessing of the same *Gott*
you wore on your buckled belt?

And what of your comrades; he of your own age
unable to rise from his roadside splint, lifting
only his head, inches from my advancing tank,
lest the last bone of blood-let youth be crushed?
And who was he, ageing, who ran through the vineyard
where Charlie took aim, life – and a sickness too?
I remember only his greylined face – and the change
in Charlie – but did not learn his name like yours.

Not a month later an ambulance driver
called the likes of you and me lucky
son-of-a-goddam-bitches to get up the front,
and offered to trade his Ronson for my belt that was yours.
The belt I later gave away with other spoils of war
but not your name, Heinz Gropsmeyer; it stayed on.
I think of us now, there where you took your *Abschied*,
green grapes under the searing *mezzogiorno* sun;
shrapnel shifting in a distant vineyard's tilth.

PAINTING IN PORT

What thoughts pervade their separate minds,
these two who share a swaying plank
above the wind and water line
of their rust-measled ship
and paint in shapes of foreign lands,
a red-lead archipelago from stem to stern?

Are they daubing over lives they've left
ashore in a native town whose name
would tumble strangely off my tongue
as Immingham off theirs?
Which brushmark hides nostalgia,
which patch obscures a home?

SHIP'S HUSBAND

You don't see his sort any more
except in certain well-worn streets
pushing his bow-wave against the brunt
of years, and blowing for a tug.
Tobacco smoke on his meerschaum skin
yellows the cheeks like old charts
of the sea bed, and his rusted brow
is grooved by the warps of time.
He rolls with a list to starboard
through constant drag of sea and net
and, if true to his own dictum, wears
a tarry marline amulet around his neck
against such ills as cannot be cured
by the rawness of onion or rum.
See him riding at anchor at the street end,
or berthed in an hour of sunshine
at an open sham-four door; look
through a parlour window to his past
and see his portrait – by *Jerome* –
in RNVR rig and silver frame
and always outboard-facing, moored alongside
a colour-tinted bride, netted
like a butterfly, ephemeral glamour.
She sees him now the way he was
and forgets to wind forward the clock.
But his memory fathoms greater depths,
lowering a lead-line to sound the seas
of childhood and the chanting school
whose echoing walls failed to out-shout
the sounds of the sea and crumbled
to the running tide of a schoolboy's mind.

He plumbs now the ebb-school hours
of slack-water evening, rippled
by eddies of fish-girls freed
in a clangor of clogs from the oak-chip
smokehouse, where a dozen restless cowls
once swung to the whim of the wind
and a lifetime's talk of splitting-knives,
of haddock-kits and tenterhooks.
Now, heaving in the plumb-line, he returns
to port, to fish-wife's tongue and pummice face,
her busy arms conger-strong and firm.
She, too, in her way, was a ruler of waves.
Sitting by the slipway of his season
provisioning the ship for wintry seas,
hoarfrost whitening his topmast truck, he
fears the black ice thickening his shrouds.

STRIKEBOUND

The ship's side gapes,
its unhealed wound still bare;
no caulker's tool
is spitting compressed air.
Where rustblood drips
from yet unplated frames
no pyrotechnic
welders sign their names.

A crane hook yawns
as with the wind it sways
and, metronomic,
whiles away its days.

WELSH ESTUARY

Like rain from the cool Welsh hills
I had come this far.
I found the hut where he had worked,
and through the wet window
saw the crumbs of words
discarded, preserved neat
and untidy on table and floor.

Below, on the ebbed-out estuary,
a grey heron, still, on a grey day;
and above, in the graveyard,
the full rhyme of grey stones
in couplets, tercets and quatrains,
end-stopped.

And behind all this,
mocking through the mist
in which a Welshman turned
my language inside out
and back to front,
the little hill, Llareggub.
There's Welsh for you.

CUCKOO

Only about once in any year
can I sling my hammock
between the greengage trunk
and apple tree, remembering
to test the non-slip knot
whose name I've quite forgotten,
stretching the canvas wide
under the fast-filling fruits,
and lie watching the shuffling leaves
piecing together a cloudless, jig-sawn sky;
or see, as now, the underbelly
of a curious thrush not long fledged
who gazes down on me; and he
may never see again such sight
as my white nest, cuckoo in his tree,
or hear, as I, from nearby dancing poplars
the swish of taffeta,
a waterfall, the sigh of one
no longer here to sigh.

TO MY WIFE...

Cloves round the ham I'd remember
and rosemary to flavour the beef.
You ask would I know how to manage
if you were the first one to die.
Manage the home? In a fashion, I'd say.
Routine? There'd be that in my life,
my goings to time and my coming back home
to find the same stillness I'd left behind
veneered with a whisper of dust.
My weekdays soothed by balsam of work.
Evenings stone-silent, only my own sad singing,
strident to reassure, just as in childhood
crossings of ghostly bedroom landings.

In our bedroom I should know cold comfort
and lonely sunbleached sheets, still
smelling the fresh-caught sea air – and you.
The bloodwarm underblanket wouldn't bring
our bed alive in love, or stilled in sleep,
and in the morning I would pour again for two,
forgetting; I'd flounder through the numbing days
to weekends' wifeless husbandry, coping,
cooking for only one reluctant appetite.
And then would be the hardest time to think,
to eat alone again, to think, and then again
the cloves round the ham I'd remember
and rosemary to flavour the beef.

SOLATIUM

It's only Sheffield plate, she would say,
but it's good and the chasing *is* by hand.
On dull afternoons she would spread old news
on the kitchen table, gather the tarnished moments
of her glinting yesterdays, upbraid them
with a gritty polish cloth blacker in parts
than her hair was grey, and I would marvel
such a dirty rag of cast-off vest
should brighten up her day so.

Stubborn pieces, like leaves on the epergne,
she'd give a harsher reprimand; verdigris
she'd even spit on, indelicately as a woman would.
Always the tray was left till last,
punished with the darkest patch of rag
and more elbow grease than all the rest,
breathed on in echo of orgasmic gasps
and titivated with the floral flannelette
of a long discarded nightdress.

After, humming a tune from Tauber, waltzing,
waiting while the kettle boiled
she would chassé the tray to the light,
mirror its gleam in her face glowing
warm where the copper showed through,
and the canary in its high sprung cage
would start again to sing.
It's only a Roller hen, she would say,
but it's company and it *has* a good song.

SONNET: THROUGH MOTHER'S EYES

In celebration of the successful cornea-grafting operation performed, shortly after mother's death, using her eyes in the restoration of sight to someone unknown.

An ear for music, eye for pretty sights
were gifts she'd share with anyone who cared.
She gave a rhythm to the spoken word
and lent her eyes to brighten starless nights;
she saw life's colours, not mere blacks and whites,
perceived a peacock in the plainest bird,
lit optic beacons when her joy was stirred
by children's songs or colourbox delights.

She showed her gratitude in later years,
bequeathed her eyes that others might see still,
and I'm aware, as I soliloquize,
that though my words may fail to reach her ears,
by some coincidence — and surgeon's skill —
my poem might be read through mother's eyes.

THIS DAY DAWNING

EFFECTS

A mild evening
of a man.
After he died
the daughter came,
a March draught
to his house.

The rooms held
small time
in bereavement.
Doors banged, lino
lifted, silverfish
went under.

Drawers, cupboards
gave up history:
buttonstick, *Sporting Pink*,
gold hunter and albert.
Slippers for the tip,
longjohns to jumble.

His *sanctum sanctorum* —
bellybrace, gimlets,
rabbeting planes —
bought the coffin in oak.
Gift to the Rifle Club
his point-two-two.

The house breathes
fresh, every corner.
Windows stare out
where gnats dance
like fountain balls
at a shooting gallery.

INTAKE

*"...at o-sixhundred hours tomorrow the bugler will march onto the
barrack square; the moment he draws in his breath to blow reveille, I
want to see every last manjack of you out of bed..."*

Sgt. Stokes, K.O.Y.L.I., 10.08.1941

Soon they had all gone,
senior form idols, conscripts,
volunteers, elder brothers
who had always led the way;
their crowded trains
like millepedes in distress.

Parents and lovers waving
them out of sight, turned,
linking arms into the blackout,
back home without a word. Gone.
And there was nothing then
for us but follow.

This is your number, write home
and tell it them, stamp it on
all your kit, your brain,
your dreams, turnings in the night;
cling fast to it at dawn;
as the sun goes down remember it.

We interpreted their trail
of spent cases, jerrycans,
brewed-up tanks and trucks,
closing with an enemy we knew
only as black lines marked on maps.

No moment, clearly defined,
told us when we shared
our brothers' war,
nor did we think to speak of it
when next we met, strangers
on the far side of years.

One certainty survives:
when the bugler moistens his lips
for The Last Post, those numbers
spring to attention, beating,
by the time it takes to draw breath,
the first chill note.

INTERLUDE

"Stand to, the old guard,
the new guard's come.
Don't care a bugger
what the new guard's done" —
but we'll have to imagine the bugle,
the band has moved on to Vienna.
Some of the men, left here
with no longer a war to fight
and not yet allowed to go home,
are assigned to mount guard
over a dump of coal
on the docks at Trieste
— anything to keep up morale.

"Take me back to Benevento
where the bints are cinquecento..."

Military procedures, duty orders,
the signing of inventories
give way to talk of prices,
going rates and market trends.
Hybrids flourish on the ashes of war:
mercato nero, barter, one currency
for twice its value in another;
chocolate for a child's birthday;
chastity for a perfumed bath;
cigarettes to a dying man with asthma.
The sentry sings, *ad nauseam*, in his box,
a squaddies' version of *'Sorrento"*
against the date of his demob.

A CHAT WITH SUSAN

Jacobo Timerman was editor of an Argentine newspaper. In 1977 he was arrested by the military government and held in solitary confinement. During interrogation his torture included the application of electric shocks: these sessions were referred to, by his custodians, as having "a chat with Susan". After two and a half years of being moved from prison to unidentified prison, he was released and exiled to Israel.

Not long in my new, dark place,
a few days perhaps, and nights
I slept propped against the wall,
half clear of the wet floor.

The cell I left had a hole
in the ground through which
to defecate. Here, I must wait
for the guard. Blindfold, I am led

to a latrine I never see.
Sometimes the guards misguide me.
It is their game. Today
they ignore my need and I am

left with my own stench
and the cold, stone floor.
There is a peephole in the door
but I'm not to see it open;

when the guard comes I must
turn my back on the door.
He takes my fouled clothes
for washing, and I see the futile

count of time on his watch
that I once wore. I am naked.
Time is an oppressive thread
stretched between talks with Susan.

Afterwards, there is no pain,
only the endless strand ravelling
and clearing, tightening sometimes
until I think that it might snap.

Today I ask to have my clothes.
They are not dry, I am told,
because it is raining. I search
down the thread for the feel

of rain, and am frightened
by the nothing that I find.
Tonight I am reclothed.
A guard, against the rules,

has left the peephole open.
I peer out into the pain
of light beyond the door.
At first I cannot see, but then

two doors . . . . a full view
of two doors, a celebration
of space . . . .
I thought, at first, it was

a trap, your eye watching
from the spyhole opposite.
I stepped back, expecting . . . . .
but when they didn't come

I dared to look once more,
then quickly turned away,
and then . . . . again.
And you were doing the same

until we paused, stared,
and shared the silent yoke
of time. You blinked.
I distinctly saw you blink.

I remember, now, that night
we spent together, the strange
game of blindman's buff we played:
peep, and move away . . . .

peep, and move away; our sense
of triumph when we synchronized;
mutual immortality. The love.
Perhaps . . . . . . you were a woman . . . ?

Yes, I clearly recall, once,
just before they came, you rubbed
your nose, slowly, against the peephole,
giving me your caress.

ASSIGNATION

It's not, dear Death, that I'm afraid to meet
you yet, but rather that I'd like to be
prepared, you know, leave nothing incomplete,
have time to dot my 'i's, to cross each 't'
and tidy up my final manuscript —
(the sneaking thought occurs that I might then
make late amendments, even have it ripped
to shreds, beg time to write it all again).
It's not that I'm afraid of you at all,
no, just that all the deaths I've known have left
so much unsaid, unchronicled, the small
important things; and guilt in those bereft.
       I do not ask that you defer my day
       but Death, do send me first your e.t.a.

TIMEKEEPER

Factory-made and tested, he wears
escapement where his heart would be;
seven-day chronometer in sealed case,
shockproof. Robot ahead of his time.

In youth, he was the one who never
questioned that the world was round
or touched to prove the paint was wet.
His monotonous chime today, cliché.

Trusted and ignored, equally, by management,
he is reliable and unintelligent
as a lighthouse, the rock on which it stands,
guarding the Company's stock of hours.

Out and about before the blind of fog
comes down, he anticipates tree-falls,
traffic-jams; the driven snow clears a path
for his car whose battery never runs flat.

He is not caught out by British Summer Time,
depolarized by jet-lag, nor, so far as
the oldest man in the works can recall,
have his grandmothers yet been interred.

Plain fact about him is, his family knows
no crises. He has the fortune of few friends
and, contrary to popular allegation,
documentary knowledge of his father.

FITTER

He wears the coarse cloth cap
of a Russian poet, or a pout-lipped
fashion model; his overalls, untouchable,
reflect the dark like a radar screen.

Most of his tools he has borrowed
and it's doubtful they'll be returned.
You've never seen the badger's bum
he's reputedly as rough as.

You'd not choose him in a shipwreck,
but you could very well be wrong.
Should the lifeboat engine fail to start
or fall apart, he'd be your man.

He'd shuffle the pieces like Scrabble,
rebuild, using four-letter words — coax,
ease the engine into life with tales
of his sea-going time and brothels in B.A.

He does not take discipline kindly. *Rules,*
he repeats, *are for the observance of fools*
and the guidance of wise men, take my word.
You can see facets of yourself in him.

Rambler, angler, wildfowler when he's free,
he knows widgeon and the flight of lapwings,
hears the blackbird writing the score for dawn
above the plainsong of the wind.

BILGE-DIVER

The acoustics of a double-bottom tank
or smokebox top are Caesar's
Palace to his Sinatra,
his shift-long repertoire
from *Nancy* to *My Way*,
his applause the chipping-hammer.

'Cleaner' is his euphemism,
paraffin and cotton-waste
his daily bread. Filthy,
he crouches beneath floorplates,
bales out the bilges
with a found tin.

He sweats, without change of costume,
through encores, singing to no-one
else listening until, in perfect time,
his cabaret ends with the four o'clock day.
In his bathroom tonight he will cut
a new best-selling single.

CANTEEN ASSISTANT

She arrives for work by taxi
she and three others
have filled with smoke.

Two years from school her wedding,
pregnant; a stillbirth, the marriage
guttered and went out.

One CSE and *something in catering
perhaps?* her testimonial; ten years on
and she'd like to go back.

She knows far more now of sickness
which keeps her absent from work
less than most of the men she serves.

Bending to the *Bain Marie* she is,
they all agree, more attractive
than when you look her in the face.

Flag days, raffles, round robins
find her an open purse; her smile
is of itself a charity.

She, too, has her dreams, but fears
the thought of her boyfriend's return
from his oil rig in Forties Field.

Her need is not so much sex
as love, and her secret
a week overdue.

OLD BOOK-KEEPER

It is almost done, this arid stint
of balancing ambivalent extremes;
his life a double-entry system: work
a force-fed virtue, all daydreams debited.

Such are his thoughts these mornings
driving himself to his desk. It's not
so much the job he's going to
miss, as the journeying between.

Company cars with coathangers jostle
him through June and July — past
the bloodied verge where poppies persist
in taking the bend too fast — into August.

30

Pea-viners have ravaged the night fields,
stripped away the haulms leaving the green
stained soil naked, shameless into the dawn.
The first of the barley is cut, and blanched

straw rolls drunken to a taut horizon.
The sun is poised to drive a slow stake
through the thumping heart of summer.
His odyssey almost complete, he approaches

that place where the man becomes the job,
the job the man; where his aim, now,
is not so much to gain, as not to lose
respect, his Libran grip on things.

And soon he will clear his desk,
pretend not to see the collection
box on its round. He will offer
a loyalty's dregs to the shredder.

THE BOTTLE BANK

Rain, all the long night rain
and in the morning clear drops again
fall from the cap of the tall oak post,
course down the painted Pub Food sign
into the uncharitable day.

The back door opens and would close
quickly of itself, but his backside
controls the force of the spring
as he hugs to himself the cardboard box
heaped with the gossip of empties.

His face a perpetual tug-of-war
between grimace of concentration
and a disconcerting grin; his nose
and mouth, like the lachrymose sign,
cannot contain their moisture.

Skirting the pool he could walk through
if he knew its shallowness, the grin
pulls him to the bottle bank,
slides the chattering load down
his belly to his feet and victory.

He selects, with idiotic care,
first clear, then green, then brown,
holds each bottle high in its turn
with his one good hand, a keeper
feeding fish to dolphins.

Each bottle shares its poem with him:
a deal over dinner last night;
rowdy twentyfirst in half-rhymed verse;
arrangement to sleep in another man's bed;
anniversary with only the date to celebrate.

The landlord will give him breakfast
when he's done. Between the grimace
and grin he'll keep the poems' secrets.
He is a man of trust, honourable,
and honoured in his society.

OUTLOOK ON MONDAY

A windscreen glints far off
like a burner's torch, slowly
cutting the country in half.

The swollen hill holds back,
an ocean roller welded to the sky
silent, stopped in its track.

Night's tide has flensed the field,
one sheep down with footrot
hapless, like a stranded seal.

Across the way, a refuse skip
run aground, abandoned.
A neighbour swabs her doorstep,

the clothesline a farcical can-can,
incontinence knickers in chorus
high-kicking out of time.

PIED WAGTAILS

They invade your thoughts, fuss about
like waitresses to brush away the bits,
flick, pat and tidy up the pasture.

When the sky's this high or higher
you can see, from the window seat, Pickering
sitting, comfortable, in its far fold.

Below the house, in the pasture with the wagtails
gone, they have put up the Michaelmas pens,
unhurried men sniffing the air for rain.

Soon now the trucks, three tiers some,
sheep — sheep upon reluctant sheep;
ramps down to a show of backsides.

Two rough handfuls of fleece and the first
ram performs his *entrechat,* mimicked
by half of the *corps de ballet.*

Green wellington boots, cowpat-coloured suits,
bland bucolic faces; farmers bid for lots,
one against another and the rain.

Drovers, dry in the truck's safe dung-smell,
play cards for cash on the straw-bale, deal,
call, shuffle and reshuffle the pack.

Above, in Wentworth Street and Newbiggin,
chimneys stand the high terraces, sullen
spectators at an end-of-season game.

Misère ouverte. Abundance declared. Suddenly
sun on the roofs. Wagtails mottle the pantiles,
pirouette, reshuffle, bid for unseen insects.

MAGAZINES IN A WAITING-ROOM

Two hours morning and evening
they practise take-offs,
landings — circuits and bumps
within a stressed perimeter.

Birds to take attention.
Winging from table to hand
and, restless, back again,
they flutter in front of eyes

that look but do not see. Doves
presaging a pregnancy, vultures
waiting on death; pigeons
homing on repeat prescriptions.

See, they roost now, but watch
them take to the air again
when the mynah calls the next name,
from inside her cage of glass.

DUCHESS

Not quite yet anachronistic
in a freshly ironed apron,
keeping the dustbin tidy —
the carton of cress
shorn combat-close.
Everyone seems to know her
but few, perhaps, so well
her doorstep conversations.

Her chosen theme today
how the feminine is demeaned
by such as page three
and silly, long-legged girls
on television commercials
who are nothing at all
to do with the product
they purport to sell.

The doorstep edges stoned,
patch of pavement swilled,
she closes and bolts her door
and the street's brightest brassware
completes her daily statement,
her queen's speech,
her early morning protest
to the jeans-and-trainers world.

NEIGHBOURS

We greet each other using Christian names
and pass the time of day, though little more.
There's no complaint of children's rowdy games
and not a word about that banging door;

all in the garden's lovely. Well, not quite —
three gladioli hardly serve to hide
that bedspring, those old motor tyres from sight
four seasons round. And who could quite abide

this knicker-buntinged clothesline day by day
and, late at night, departing visitors
who want the world to hear them on their way,
who rev-up engines, double-slam car doors?

Then, when the neighbourhood gets back to sleep
there's always one bright spark on early shift
at six, his valedictory beep-beep
is bloody . . . . well, I'm sure you get my drift.

One irritant we've noticed recently
is where a boy stands at the backyard sink
intent to reach the highest he can pee —
his target is the windowledge, we think.

Beware, this go-go area for dogs
demands that you be careful where you put
your feet, and be forewarned that burning logs
will punctuate your paintwork with their soot.

This sitting on front doorsteps lowers the tone —
sun-bathing on the pavement's just not on —
you'd scarcely think that one would be alone
in wondering where dignity has gone.

But now the movers' men have filled the van,
our house is empty, we're about to go,
the thought occurs: throughout our three-year span
they never told us we'd annoyed them so.

CURRICULUM VITAE

Not a born leader nor a drop-out, he
is valued for his sheer utility —
state education has prepared him for
the Forces, unemployment, factory floor.

A family-allowance come of age,
they say he's fortunate to earn a wage.
Lucky be buggered! That's his father's shout,
For this we fought — the gaffers, and the Kraut.

He is the basic model as it comes
devoid of extras; he accepts the crumbs
from richer tables and he keeps his place,
homo vulgaris. Yes, you'll know the face,

he is the one who answers truthfully
researchers' questionnaires, and it is he
who pays his union dues and doesn't run
for office; reads both *Telegraph* and *Sun*.

He knows the etymology of *berk*
so doesn't use the word; he likes his work.
A wife and rented house supply his need;
between them they'll perpetuate the breed.

Successive politicians court his votes;
the Antichrist, Computer, sifts his notes,
retrieves him under (Mr/Mrs/Miss)
abbreviated, in parenthesis.

More mouse than man's a judgement one might make,
a slow beginner, hardly yet awake —
but don't be misled, all's not as it seems:
he kills the fiercest dragons in his dreams

but holds his counsel, dumb against the day
he deems the time has come to have his say
and from the literati he'll reclaim
the wealth of poems written in his name.

THE STING

Wanted, on a charge of seditious libel contained in his ironical work entitled
'*The Shortest Way With The Dissenters*' a reward of Fifty Pounds is
offered for information leading to the arrest of

Daniel Defoe

*"a middle-sized man about forty years old, brown complexion, dark brown
hair bur wears a wig: a hooked nose, sharp chin, grey eyes; a large mole
near his mouth."*

London Gazette, c1702

I suppose the mole was a dead give-away,
and money talks — it always did —
fifty pounds would have bought more
than a lot of first editions
on Grub Street in those days.

Caught, sentenced, pilloried for three days.
But the crowds came not with stones
or foul abuse; rather with words of praise
and flowers to deck the pillory,
flasks to drink your health;

money, too, to buy your written works.
Your publishers set up stalls, stood by
with reprints, saying "What a turn-up
for the book. Better this, by far,
than any ordinary signing session!"

Amen to that —

and Robinson Crusoe yet to set sail from Hull;
it makes you proud.

WORDS

Against us all
who wrong you,
won't you fight
sometimes —as the baited bull
uses horns
and skull,
when driven by pain
to retaliate —
fight back
you English words.

I know you:
you are regal as queens,
juicy as fruit,
carefree as gay,
as butch as a dame
in a man's suit;
chick as a girl,
or as queer
as the transvestite
in the heat
of the night.
It is strange how the thought
of a close-cut lawn
could lead
via grass
to smack or crack;
that a joint
can be bought
not to roast

but to smoke,
and a poke
could be other
than the bonnet once worn
by one's mother.

But it's tough
to know what is meant
by a puff,
and a bust
I'd decline
to define.

Fortify me
with some frankness
from York
whose flat-vowelled talk
has no frills,
from Grimsby and Clee
and old Ridings
where a spade stays a spade,
and invoices bills,
no less.
Let me sometimes stand
with you,
attack,
and turn my hand
against all whose aims
usurp your good names;
let us win back her wand
for the fairy.

EPITHALAMIUM

We hadn't thought to meet again
so soon after that first glance,
mutually approving, in the pub
before the dance. Introduction
superfluous. *Tuxedo Junction. In the Mood.*

I overstayed my leave, then back
to barracks; a last few tedious months
and every day our letters,
each repeating a love
that neither knew the measure of.

Late summer and I came home
to stay, to shake out a future
from the given cardboard box —
gaberdine, double-breasted
grey pinstripe and all.

And all that September we watched
the leaves re-colour our secret wood
and months later, on the bus
passing that place, you would press
your knee to mine, and it was as good.

Our wedding in April; the honeymoon.
Primroses from a Sussex wood
our epithalamium
pressed between cellophane sheets
in an album of fading fashions.

And so again to September, your dirndls
put away, the borrowed wrap-overs
letting out our secret
inch by flowered inch
to a brittle winter.

The burnished snow rejecting
my prints each evening
to your ward. Our firstborn.
The having, holding,
and the long, reluctant letting go.

ALL YOU NEED IS LOVE

They bring their children now
to see us, over the rebuilt bridges.
Something delicate, potent, in the smell
of a child's skin, his hair,
transcends time and reason.

There is joy as well as hurt,
when he tires of our game,
in his well-aimed handful of toys.
It is a phase. There were always
phases, not to be talked about.

A son's first graffito, saying
little, but significant of much.
The mass of motorbikes, summonses;
rebellion pushing the clock past midnight;
callers in cars and quiet conversations.

Posters of Paul and John, guardant
over a daughter's bed, their music
closeting her away for hours,
all you need is love pounding the walls.
Horses; the cavalletti of puberty.

Grandad, the children say, *come
into the garden and play — and Grandma.*
We count slowly up to ten, then
set out in search of them, leave
their favourite places until last,

find precisely what it is we seek.
Asleep now in his mother's warmth,
'Little Black Sambo' fallen to the floor,
they carry him into the car and are
gone with the sun, over safe bridges.

We bring the house to order, replace
the ornaments, make another pot of tea,
and know that we shall ache all week
from games we played far less
for their sakes than for our own.

BACALAO

Yesterday's boat brought a shark, hoisted
tail-over-snout above deck, tall, sleek
as stray cats scavenging the refuse bins;
sight-seers a mixed catch of language.

Today, the *Mar Celeste* has landed her fish
except these five kept by the crew for curing,
split, salted and spreadeagled between stays,
bacalao hung to the sun and the wind.

My father would have quickened to this,
envied these Mallorquin their climate,
criticised, enthused, pronounced judgement
based on a lifetime's curing of cod.

Splitting, pricking-up, laying out the fish
to dry, participles by which he lived;
he knew, by smell and feel of skin, a catch
from Iceland, White Sea, the Faroes.

Bacalao, he used to say, *a delicacy in Spain,*
steaming the biscuit-hard flakes, flavouring
the whole house, adding parsley; proving, if only
to himself, his work *food fit for a king.*

ANNIVERSARY

But then, with age, it's not at all like that,
there's not the fight to keep the fire alight
there was when we were young; and now tonight
the ash of years perpetuates the heat,
and love's become a comfortable grate
by which to sit, touch hands to consummate.

No more the backing smoke, eye-smarting haze,
or panic caused by roaring chimney fires.
Burnt out by now the vicious, spitting coals;
no bubbling hiss of tarry will-o-wisps.
A graceful, ballet-skirted glow remains
to dance the hearth's slow-burning of the days.

To think that, years ago, these coals were trees
and slender saplings wrestled with wild winds,
bowed low, sprang back and scratched the seasons' eyes
and suffered in each other's restlessness,
then, in full time, stood proud with summer's pods,
and now their progeny our favourite woods.

Today we walk through winter trees, and by
the trackside, skeletal against the sky
the silver birch, its lace all stripped away,
splendid in sunlight, seems to us to say:
though greens that autumn browned are gone today,
touch, feel my bark, the warmth is here to stay.

THE GAZEBO

Today I awoke early, restless, refusing the last
dark drops from the dugs of sleep, impatient
for the day as a mule to slip its spancel,
yet not wanting to listen again to the words

I'd heard so many times — like numbers for the rugby
league cup draw shaken in their velvet bag,
picked out in random order — always the same words.
Presentation handshake, photograph I'll likely never see,

and this final homeward journey, earlier than usual.
The books are closed. My desk, its drawers now empty,
will face tomorrow from a slightly different angle
with someone else's photograph in place of yours.

It is good, alone in the car, to savour homecoming;
the road seems to have shed its sense of urgency.
Combines have come like carrion crows to bloat
on the fattening feast; the hedgerow throws a cloak

over the place where poppies spilled their blood.
Two men with a theodolite read the field's palm,
predict a meeting with the motorway next year.
A long and happy retirement, he said. They clapped.

I heard partridge rising, shot them down with words.
You will want to know how it was; I shall have time
to tell. And while I'm telling we shall keep
one eye to the future, looking for new roads.

Rest will not contain us both for long, and if time
and fate should sometimes make us weak we shall strive,
like the skylark rising, for a song of noble note,
dip our minds into new colours in the woods again.

Too soon now I steer the car under the prunus arch
into the drive. *Piacevole*, carved in Lombardic at
the outset of our journey, weathered now but bold.
Petunias play tubas in the sawn-off buttertub.

You meet me home. We walk into the garden, sit on
the long seat and share a silent gathering of strength.
We'll have tea on the lawn, perhaps, and talk of endings
and beginnings, and one of us will fall asleep.

Tomorrow we shall blow dust off old plans. There
will be York stone to cut, edges crisp as cinder-toffee.
You will serve a brave new recipe for lunch. And after,
we shall build the gazebo where our dreams are stored.

THIS DAY DAWNING

This day dawning is the black fruitgum,
the sixpence in the pudding; the day
dad first let go the bicycle's saddle.
It is my mother's knee, the ease
when the toothache had gone.

It is the day I was appointed —
and the day I was released.
It is every bill in the house paid off.
This day is cyclamen and holly
dancing to a daffodil band.

It is the day when Olive said *yes*.
Bubbles in a baby's bath, balloons
and his first bouncing words.
It is the day my son returned home;
my daughter singing in the choir.

It is the Christmas stockings filled;
the tightly rolled-up fiver
in the Salvation Army tin.
Top hat and tails and taxis
and that first successful waltz.

It is Pickering Park and Costello;
one magnificent minnow
in a jam jar bright with rainbows.
It is the uncashed cheque for one guinea
for a first ever poem in print.

This day dawning is the taste returning
after a bout of heavy cold.
It is the irresistible invitation
of a vast untrodden snow
and only I can put my foot in it.

LOVE STORY

Their wedding holds firm
in its frame on the wall —
above the gravid shelves
of Bainbridge, Yevtushenko —
the frontispiece
of an ageing book.

Take down their tome
and read how forty years
taught tolerance, timing,
routine — even *ad libs*
are polished with practice,
though their style is spare.

Barely a word they waste
and their silences
say more for them.
Apart, they are closer
than together, knowing by heart
each other's conflating rôle;

she, in the kitchen,
slicing and halving the loaf
— diagonally on Sundays —
Mondays, giving the house
and him no rest,
blowing out her gale;

he, in the garden shed,
chewing an endless cud
of self-control, feeding
a rodent anger,
poulticing with pastimes
the unspent rage of his youth.

Evenings, a shared synopsis,
a tautology of sighs . . . .
And now their kiss goodnight
asks no new question,
makes no fresh statement
as would its absence.

Their story's not yet over —
leave them in this lacuna,
put their book back on its shelf
beneath the faded photo
of two young lovers —
each watching the other grow old.

LOVE IS A FOUR-LETTER WORLD

THE LIGHT OF THE WORLD

a Holman Hunt print remembered

Taller than I'd first imagined Jesus;
nor could I then be certain
the expression on his face
changed as light from his lamp

fell through tall cow-parsley
to the bare feet I feared for
on such harsh ground;
his hand knocking at the door.

His eyes tired, sad perhaps
as if he, too, would have preferred,
like my elder brother,
not to be made to share

a bedroom with a boy
so young who daily broke
the unfair tenth commandment
on such as seniority,

a waistcoatful of pockets,
full-length baggy flannels
and heavy-soled brown brogues.
And Brylcreemed hair

parted, sleek as the flakes
of kippers our father boned
when mother took them out
from the fireside oven

in brittle back-numbers
of *Hull Daily Mail*
cooked bronze as the kippers.
The hot, glazed bed-brick

she'd wrap and carry upstairs
to the foot of our bed
under the watchful eyes of Jesus.
My brother, two hours later to bed,

offering my offending socks
with his prayer to the night air,
trapping them under the sash.
Neither forgiving my trespass.

PETER'S HOUSE

Peter's house was different.
No father home each evening
from the docks; an uncle
occasionally from sea.
There we could feel free.

Like when his uncle Jack
brought home the parrot.
'African Grey', he had said,
'screech like a windlass brake,
but can't get the bugger to talk.'

'Should have had its tongue
split with a sixpenny piece
when the bugger was young',
his uncle Jack had said.
One morning the parrot lay dead.

Landing in Hull, late summer,
he'd brought a chameleon.
Aloof, it had held a still pose
on top of the curtain pole —
it was there when we came in from school:

Peter, his uncle and I had caught flies
and pulled off one of their wings,
sent them climbing in range of its tongue;
'like feeding a donkey strawberries',
his uncle Jack had said, 'it is.'

And not very long after that
Peter's house had been ripped
from its roots by a bomb,
and I heard that his uncle Jack
had gone down off Murmansk.

TUTORIAL

What can I say of her face? It was all
of a smile; hair done in a tight-pinned bun;
her bosom ample, indeterminate.
Ageless, she had lived in this room always.

Her skirt wide, almost, as it was long,
you had to stand behind to see at all
the bentwood chair she sat on.
She was the sort that people came to.

Her gold-tipped teeth a fascination
glimpsed in the gas-light's surge
when the mantle prattled. She rummaged
in the chiffonier, its dark drawer of memories

and playing-cards, found the harmonica —
repaired at one end with a sharp twist
of wire saved from a firewood bundle.
It was a lesson in a simple language:

'blo-ow suck blo-ow suck blo-ow blow blo-ow',
teaching a boy's bloomed lips to mouth
her favourite and only tune
in a camphorated key of 'C'

in the dim-lit room, with her smile,
the gold, the spittle that they shared
and the one discordant reed
that made the song their own.

THE COD FARM

I have your photo on my wall
in grainy not-quite-black-and-white,
blown-up, to try to bring you close

the way few sons and fathers are.
The original's in Hull museum —
The Cod Farm: you, flat cap and all,

with cod spread out on racks to dry
salt-white, 'earning a crust' by which
Mum bought that first school uniform

I rolled around the playground in
to make less obviously new
to boys with bigger fists than mine.

'See Maurice, see our Dad again!'.
Quite what the others find of you
in me, they don't explain. Bald head;

the less than generous mouth; your voice?
And I don't tell them how I feel
a certain late affinity;

how, since you died, sometimes it seems
it's not my face but yours I shave
(though wrong way round); your faults I see

mirrored in me — like how I use
codology the way you did
for blowing up reality

in grainy not-quite-blacks-or-whites
to hold on to a love I fear
to lose, or maybe never had.

SOLITAIRE

i.m. Maud Evelyne and Evelyn

Sometime before the start of World War One
there must have been a day when all their pride
reflected from the facets of one stone,
claw-mounted, on an eighteen-carat ring.
And later, newly wed, they would have stood,
she, with a centre-parting, combed-back hair
and he, head high, in stiff wing-collared shirt,
braced for the photograph's magnesium flare.

Filial wistfulness would beg the lie
that marriage, war, attrition of the years
exacted equal toll from each, but truth
insists that this was not the case, and cites
their ring she gave to me before she died,
its shank worn thin, the diamond vivified.

WOMAN IN THE CROWD

for Jean, in a slow winter

Your Mum and I down town —
new mall, old marketplace —
and in the shifting crowd
briefly, perhaps your face,
deportment, hair.

Two youngsters of your own,
with half a lifetime gone,
your home a world away
from home and moving on.
Yet here you are

where albums hold you still
freeze-framed along the years;
your paintings in our hall;
your laughter, letters, tears
wring in locked drawers;

and sometimes, in the folds
of dreams, a daughter's call —
we waken to your name —
a known kick on the wall
of the spent womb.

IN VACUO

I keep them in this box which used to house
five units each of fifty carbon sheets —
your postcards: Pyramids, the Nile and Dhows;
Playa de Palma; cafés on the streets

of Paris; gaudy panoramic views
from Naxos where you made a second home.
'Brazil is beautiful — I'm on a cruise
along the Amazon.' 'With love from Rome.'

In what we'd neither of us claim has been
a close relationship, these cards fill gaps;
each brings the beating of shared blood. Each scene
initiates a survey of my maps:

I pinpoint Casablanca — 'Oh, the heat!',
place Tarbert out on Harris — '…blowing hard…',
and trace the many places where we meet
in words behind the gloss of each kept card

then hoard them tightly packed inside their box,
in vain to prove that your propensity
for travelling supports the paradox
of distance closing to propinquity.

LOVE OF AN AUTUMN AFTERNOON

September sunshine cuts a wedge of green
and lays the cypress tree three times its length
along the lawn; the honeysuckled air
invigorates — like coming out from school.
It's on such afternoons as this I mean
to tell you of my love, how much its strength
has grown with time; to lean across your chair
and touch, and kiss you, lightly, hoping you'll
respond. And so I do — and you do, too,
and now our autumn's warm and green and gold.
True, there are days, not many but a few,
when friendliness and love remain untold,
but on such afternoons as this it's fair
to say there's nothing that we two won't share.

MRS. CHOLMONDELEY

Squeaks of a dry-hinged gate,
or a wren scourging
a gap in the hedge
and I'm back that afternoon
pruning clematis
where it fingered sky
at the Bramley's tips.

'Sweet-and-sour', you'd said,
remember, planting it there
under the cankered tree,
young roots tracing old,
puddling them in.

63

It was a wren bullied
the blood-red sun
that afternoon, secateurs
keen as the bird's fiat;
pain, bitter-sweet, just
this side of fainting;
a pistachio of fingertip —
somewhere my prints on the soil —
and spent coins of blood
up the garden path
to the kitchen sink.
Two months and more
Tipp-exed misprints,
nine-finger typing.

Squeals of a snatching brake,
or a wren chivvying
summer rain:
Mrs. Cholmondeley, pale blue
bleeding to mauve,
crêpe fingering sky again.

COMFORTS

Come back soon to a real Bridlington welcome
— noticeboards on the main roads out.

Those holidays, our nineteen-twenties
parents freed us here, their skinny kids
in handknit woollen swimsuits —
crotches like anglers' landing-nets —
peeing a catch of seawater
between sun-toughened knees;
and schooldays following, bubblegums
of skin peeled from our shoulders
pagefuls of rubbings-out.
Retirement brought us back to spend
the nineties, perhaps to close our book
in the comfort of this place.

But now we find that holidays
mean all the parking spaces filled;
we're jostled off the pavements
by macro-bosoms from McGill,
ogled by Cyclops beer-guts,
leered at by anal cleavages
escaping from Bermudas;
we're tripped by men in sandals
and obligatory black socks;
there's cellulite in armfuls here
and all the very ones who 'really shouldn't'
force-feed each other burgers.

From Sheffield, Bradford, Barnsley most,
the locals call them Comforts, for the way
they say they've 'come for t'day'.
And when they've 'done us brass' and driven off
westward past the come-back signs —
to the wife's part-time, the old man's emphysema —
what they leave behind for us
(discounting all the parking bays
of dunked-out teabags, disposables and stubs)
is the comfort of a season's end
in open space, the scour of rough seas
and the culling winds of winter.

LESSONS IN AGE

We sit in facing chairs and share an hour
or so of silence, then both speak at once
our thoughts — 'I'll put the kettle on.' 'I'll draw
the curtains.' — or reel off some household tip:

'A bunch of rhubarb leaves brought to the boil
will clean stained pans as good as anything.'

'To change a fuse-wire, first switch off the mains —
and don't forget the torch that's hanging there
should have its batteries renewed each year.
The fuseholder with white spots is for lights —
5 amps — the thinnest fuse-wire on the card.'

So much to learn; so much to leave behind.
Against the time one's left to sit alone
we've planned our strategy, reversing roles
to learn each other's skills.

'For smooth white sauce
first make a roux: a knob of margarine,
a saucepan on low heat, the cooking-spoon
of cornflour — not too heaped, mix to a paste;
add milk, bring gently ... well, you know the rest,
but keep on stirring — use the whisk — you'll feel
the thickening in time.'

　　　　　　　　　And when our time
is up, no doubt they'll say we blended well,
and so we do, but we have problems too —

well, don't we all? Compatibility
does not come cheap, and this late in our lives
we daren't allow ourselves the luxury
of good old-fashioned rows — too great the risk
before we'd made it up time might be called.

'The wrench to turn the stopcock's in the space
below the sink — clockwise for *off*. Make sure
the central-heating boiler's switched off first.'

Our 1940's closer than last year
and love grows more demanding as we age:
protectiveness and bossiness encroach
to silt the veins where lust once ran in spate —

'Not with the teacloth — use the oven-gloves.'

'That way you'll hurt your back — lift from the knees.'

So much to leave behind; so much to learn.

SOLSTICE

i.m. E.D.

Low-angled sun shines through our window and
the tinsel-decorated room glows bright
this shortest day. The photo in my hand
records a day of summer: you, in white

or off-white outfit, champagne shoes and bag,
sit, smiling, on the grass; below's the date
of nineteen-eightythree — before the drag
of wolflike illness bowed you with its weight.

The Christmas card (which brought this happy you,
your Michael kindly sent us so that we
remember you the way you'd want us to)
he's annotated, not with elegy

but with a celebration of your life
and of your poems read in Requiem,
of joyful times you'd shared as man and wife;
its scene depicts Christ's birth at Bethlehem,

a Tintoretto print, which might have been
precisely of your choice, as though you'd known
we'd need such crutch of hope on which to lean.
The card is signed in Michael's name alone.

REMNANTS

Another year to slough like an old suit
rancid with sweat and sundry spillages,
congealing loves, and hatreds undeclared;
baggy from overnighting with intent
where dreams disintegrate in face of dawn –
and just becoming comfortable, warm.

With each year-end we play out this charade
as though some evil curse would strike us down
if, just for once, we dared sneak off to bed
and leave the old clothes crumpled on the floor
before the minute-hand eclipsed the hour-
hand's upright poise. And so we catnap here

a last few hours, for auld lang syne. The box
repeats repeats long past their drowse-by date –
climactic highlights, schmaltz and instant-sex
and holidays abroad we can't afford,
then rendezvous with Scotland and the malt,
the kilts that leave us cold, bagpipes that don't –

until, due deference done to Hogmanay,
past midnight we switch off the set, undress,
let fall the good old days, shrug off the bad,
but don't discard them all: a few we'll keep
like scraps of tweed cut off with pinking-shears,
and buttons saved from cast-offs through the years.

PILLOW-TALK

It troubles me how, recently
we've grown

apart, and don't now share,
as once we did,

that perfect empathy
we made our own

in so relaxed a way.
I cannot rid

my mind of fears and doubts
which come between

us now.
You seem so distant when I try

to reach you;
it's as though somehow I've been

rejected, bypassed,
and I don't know why.

Our intimacy's lately lost
all zest

and when we touch
it's only for a little while –

I can't remember when
we two caressed

in any lasting way.
Please make me smile

again, for old time's sake,
please say you'll keep

a tryst, and share my bed tonight,
dear Sleep.

AUTUMN LODGE — THE DAYROOM

They try to read beyond each other's eyes
but only see a face's fallen shape,
the balding eyebrows and the nasal hair,
the fissures of a deeply sculpted frown,
the corners of a mouth slow-arcing down;

each sees in each the portraiture of age
beyond her own, and wonders how it feels
to be as frail as one across the room
who, standing now, extends an arm to me
and helps me from my chair, and in to tea.

EX LIBRIS

Have you seen them, the silly old chumps?
If the library opened at dawn
they'd be there with their coughs and their limps
a good fifteen minutes before.

Have a look how they queue at the door
ten minutes to opening-time,
date-stamped and dog-eared and worn
like the books they're about to return.

Their addiction to standing in queues
was born in their boring old war:
up the blue, for their soyas and 'V's;
on the Home Front, for something to wear.

It's a kind of group statement they make —
it's not only for books that they come —
standing here they are making their mark,
being noticed, a someone, a name.

There's a nexus slipped out of their lives
and they seek to recapture it here
swapping wartime exploits and lost loves —
all that bull about *esprit de corps*.

When the door is unbolted at ten,
like good soldiers they'll pick up their bags,
put their war snaps away and file in
to search for their dead in new books.

O TEMPORA! O MORES!

Girls bursting out
from Headlands High
are switched on,
plugged in to
themselves.
A peripatetic
takes it out
on his clutch
and blitzes
his sunroof
with bassbeat.

It's all *pleases* and *pardons*
in our pensioners' café
and muzak restful
as the *Jesu Joy* of the Crem;
a hearing-aid howls now and then.
Nobody's looking
but everyone's watching
the couple who've lingered
too long at the one window table.
When they stand up to leave
it's Klondike.

A VIEW OF THE SEA

Las Cascadas, Puerto de Andraitx, Majorca

Steep, you'd have to call this coastline;
the houses, grafted to the island's bone,
white as gulls' wings, except when seen
form a gull-high view: oven-hot peach

and terracotta pantile roofs
cascade to the cool of the sea.
It is good, like watching others at work,
to gaze, from this honeysuckled balcony,

upon comings and goings below, although
the boats are too far off to be peopled
like the houses ashore. From my seat
in a slant of shade I become absorbed.

Garrulous in second, a Volkswagen grows
slowly bigger up the terraced hill, pulls
into position centre-stage, and stops;
the engine clears its throat, then dies.

Car doors open – his and hers – and shut
with a positive Doppelpunkt:
they walk to the rear as to part
wordless, hesitate, turn, touch hands

and kiss, lightly, their bodies held
apart – I can see the sea between.
Watching them their separate ways
I'm left to guess their story.

Whatever, they will both live it out
unknowing my concern, not even caring.
My theories cascade to the pull of the sea,
compelling, misting now, indeterminate.

MOMENT IN HISTORY

Chesters, Hadrian's Wall, 1992

All day he smothers her with lore –
has done for years. Now it's *Cilurnum*,
stone footings of a Roman fort,

carved gulleys, good-luck phallus.
Drowns her now with pleasures,
all imagined, in The Baths ...

Frigidarium ...

        Tepidaria ...

                Caldaria ...

She doesn't hear. She's sloughing
the wersh remains of him,
awaiting her moment to tell ...

... not here, in the peopled museum,
his hymning the glass-cased remains
and chanting aloud to found stones:

... millefiori brooch ... jet ring ...
snaffle bit ... entrenching tool ...
To the goddess Fortuna, Conservatrix ...

They'll take English tea on a bench
in the afternoon sun and she'll tell
of her lover. He'll jet back

alone to Tacoma.

SKULLS AT PHNOM PENH

The road here reaches
back from the grave,
man-laid, each cobble
stares you out
from its two dark vaults.

No need of necromantic art
to bring alive
the unspoken words.
The cobbles whisper,
conch-like, in the wind:

you could have cared;
you should have cared.

ONCE MORE, ON WAR

1. GAME CALL

Best part of half a century since last
we'd met. Old Corporal Barry he was then
to us young soldiers; must have been at least
twelve years my senior, an ancient man,

survivor of Tobruk, Sidi Rezegh –
those battles that the wireless used to name
and we'd seen spelt out in the local rag –
Gazala, Fort Capuzzo, Bir Hakeim.

Such place-names filled our conversations then
before I was myself posted abroad
to join his unit under canvas on
the desert's edge near Cairo. As I said,

not far off fifty years and now I faced,
just by the baker's shop in my new town,
a man I thought I recognized – the eyes
perhaps, or something of the nose, then soon

the angle of his head convincing me
I knew him from somewhere. He showed no sign
of recognition, so, reluctantly
I passed him by – but turned to look again

and saw a walk that leapt across the years,
a march I knew I first fell in behind
at Beni Yusef, with the IVth Hussars.
I rushed back – 'Barry!', offering my hand

but even though he shook it in return,
he couldn't place my name, nor did my face
strike chords. He'd 'stopped one in the Gothic Line',
(I knew) 'and can't remember much these days.'

'The Regiment, and Colonel Kidde (Sunray),
Lance Sergeant Dunne ...' and some before my time
he could recall, but not remember me,
remustered Driver/Op fresh out from home,

until I asked him did he still play Bridge,
(We'd once played partners). Well, that took the trick –
the Slam was on! – with 'Charlie Ryde ... Bill Budge ...'
an outspread groundsheet, and that grubby pack.

2. SNAKES IN SICILY

The skin once scratched, old desert-sores began
once more to itch, and so we met again
and told conflicting versions of events;
compared the turns our lives had taken since.

He showed me photographs. On two of them
I could identify myself for him
and name some others he could not recall.
He had some German photographs as well,

he'd 'found them in a Jerry, a Mark Three,
shot-up outside – let's think – Mersah Matruh':
a group of Panzer troops; a girl back home
in German snow – we couldn't say her name,

but could read *Schlangen auf Sizilien*
written in ink on the reverse of one
cracked photograph. These snakes in Sicily
evoked that snake which came one hot, hot day

to drink while Lawrence at his water trough
stood like a second-comer, wondering if
his fear, or fear of being cowardly
would make him kill the drinker where it lay;

these half a dozen dead snakes in the dust
seemed somehow symptomatic of war's waste,
of chances missed. I'd say Lawrence was right –
here, too, was pettiness to expiate.

More than a month now and the dreams persist
of troops and tanks, and bodies in the dust;
I, in pyjamas, have the killing-stick,
the fear, the cowardice, a drinking snake.

ALL DOWN THE AVENUE

All down the avenue the houses make
bold statements, fantasize: first, Number 2,
with scarlet lamps and phallic Irish yew,
proclaims *Retirement Home for Gentlefolk.*

Then, over by the disused petrol pump
there's *Vindolanda,* double-glazed and lagged:
clearly the house is old, its ridgepole sagged,
but nothing here suggests a Roman camp.

Greengables lies a midlength terrace-house.
Next-door's *The Lindens*: not a lime in sight,
unless we count the floodlighting at night;
(that half-shut stable-door's not for a horse).

Cartref, oh, yes, *Cartref*! You're sure to meet
a *Cartref* every hundred homes or so:
St. David's songs left this one years ago
when Mamgu's health declined in Pontypridd.

Broadacres! What imaginative flair
led to the christening of 26,
whose aspect offers only others' bricks
plus, on a cloudless day, St. Mary's spire?

How precious are the dreams which move the mind
to sublimate what's ugly, bland or trite;
yet time might prove the incomers were right
renaming *Sunrise Cottage*: *Journey's End.*

HALF-TERM

An hour into our shopping trip I flag,
my threshold reached, and leave her to her quest
for 'something colourful but not too young,
to wear to next month's golden wedding do',
escaping to this seat out in the mall.

Here, while my wife re-racks the whole boutique,
I sit and watch the well-dressed shoppers pause
to gaze in windows, some at the displays
and some to titivate their scarf or hat
or satisfy a narcissistic need.

And if you've ever wondered what goes on
inside the heads of men who sit on seats
and ogle passers-by, come, sit with me,
it's marvellous – fantastic's more the word!
I choose at will, make this one rich, that poor –

they run a Merc or Mini at my whim;
this man's done time; that woman's on the stage;
he, in the Crombie, hosts a pheasant shoot;
she's not his wife; this rather plump girl sings
contralto; and this one … this is my wife –

she hasn't bought a dress. 'Couldn't decide
between the paisley two-piece and a warm
more serviceable jersey-cloth. Half-term,
you see', she says, 'the shops are full of kids
whose mothers let them do just as they like

and I get flustered, then can't concentrate.
We'll come again, when schools are back ...', she jerks
me back into the school of mundane thought –
and this ménage à trois, that unfrocked priest,
this fool, re-metamorphose and move on.

ONLY CONNECT

for John Lucas

One canvas calls
whenever I'm in Hull:
lack-literate,
I'm drawn to Bundy's *School*

ceilinged in smoke
and dole of candlelight
where workworn men
first learn to read and write;

one sits alone,
looks apprehensive, grim
and out of place:
I see myself in him

and can't equate –
a century ahead –
my workthrift years
with all the books unread.

My passion primed,
I reach to you and send
a postcard print
and you respond, 'Dear friend,

this brush speaks well
alongside Tawney's pen!
Enclosed: his words.'
The lamps are lit again.

THE HULL POETS – AND PIGEONS

'... the third generation Hull poets are proving worthy inheritors of the Larkin-Dunn estate.'

John Osborne on *The Hull Poets*
Lincolnshire & Humberside Arts' *Arts Diary*
Jan-Feb 1987

But few of them are native to the town,
most came by chance, or maybe second choice
and some have taken off with good degrees;
others fillet fish, or sign for dole.
One I know who flew the nest southwards
is honoured now, well-known and widely read
but yet unclaimed by Hull, his native town.
Such recognition isn't easily
obtained in Hull – the opportunity
might come with death: few Hullites there can be
who're unaware of Marvell's old complaint

83

to his coy lady, voiced by Humber's tide
above the sound of time's winged chariot;
but fewer still will know that Stevie Smith
lived here her early, valuable years.

Hull City Hall's a favoured pigeon squat
and Queen Victoria's monument is not
amused by small excretions, year on year;
by columnists and poets home to roost,
perhaps to earn, in time, the town's acclaim,
be granted all the privilege and pomp
the Three Crowns coat-of-arms would guarantee;
but clap your hands in Queen Victoria Square –
indigenous pigeons take to the air,
while alien poets are named as legatees
to Halls of Residence in Cottingham
and Bransholme's sprawling council house estates.
It matters not at all from where they came,
the pigeons or the poets; *poems* remain –
well, some – and pigeon-muck accumulates.

Were I a pigeon I'd have lost my strut,
revisiting a Humberside library,
to find my own slim volume credited
not to me, *Maurice,* but to *Margaret*,
denying me, whilst not my place of birth,
my rightful gender – hitting where it hurts –
(and Margaret's fame required no boost from me!).
And so I doubt Hull's City Fathers will
remark the passing of one *Rutherford*,
son of a hull fish curer's manager
and writer of occasional short verse,

84

but should you see, one day, a chequered-blue
chance-bred streeter, in weak iambic flight,
homing on Hull like some lost poem recalled,
make room along the ledge – and let it land.

LIME STREET TO PARAGON

returning from a meeting with poets

Slowing for Batley
I'm reading a poem
of someone who'd fallen
asleep on a journey
reading a poem.

The poem was dreaming
a poem of someone
who'd fallen asleep in
a poem unwritten

till slowing for Batley

woke me.

ON SAVING THE NON-WINNERS PILE FOR
RE-USE AS DRAFT-PAPER

Some became almost friends
you wouldn't want to lose;
but some were just too nice
to be believed.

One wore pale pink – and didn't wash.

The weaker ones brought sick-notes
they'd salvaged from Eng. Lit.,
or piggybacked on Old Masters.

Some had been allowed too slack a rein, taken the bit and
over-run.

A few had been on courses
for advanced assertiveness.

Some weren't decided on a form
until halfway, then limped home in
iambics and tetrameters.

One, acrobatic, did handstands
& leapfrogged over ampersands.

Among first persons singular
one towered over all the rest
by sneaky use of lower-case.

Time warp incarcerated some
in outworn cloaks and hats of yore
to twixt and tween lost schooldays o'er.

Still more were cut by scattered shards
and bled in rosebay willowherb
or plashed through skeins of gossamer
to where they all arrived to meld
poetical as palimpsest.

THE READING

His beard has practised
all week without a comb.
He shuffles through
a well-thumbed sheaf
of poems – massed

endpapers for the one
he's brought to read.
Selfish with his foreplay
he describes
his poem's conception,

relives its long gestation.
All, then, that remains
is for him to read the thing.
Listen, and you'll hear
Movement, Dylan, Martian,

then, somewhere hereabouts
he finds for what it's worth
the voice he likes
to call his own ...
now, coming

to his *coup de grâce*
he hones to bare bone
colloquial modernity,
no skulker behind euphemism
he; but he fails

by eschewing the use
of a northern 'u' as in duck,
both vowel and impact weaken
pronounced more like quack.
The poem is born deformed.

His friend in the fourth row
slaps it into life;
motherless it cries
for sympathy and understanding.
Catharsis is complete.

The beard leads its poet
off the stage.
They'll ask you
what it was he read.
You won't remember.

DEAR MR. GEORGE

'It would be idle to claim that this pupil's record in most subjects is all that an educational institution would desire, but he has done very careful and good work in Typewriting. This suggests that he has a leaning towards the practical rather than the theoretical side of work. He will probably perform good service for an employer, and I know from experience that he will always be courteous, and regular and punctual in attendance.'

Allan F. George LL.B., B.Sc. (Econ.) Lond.
Principal, City of Hull College of Commerce
12.04.1938

Dear Mr. George, your words are with me yet,
outlasting fully fifty years in which
I've, probably, performed good services
for more than one employer, none of whom
I deigned to show your Testimonial.

It would not be at all idle to claim
that irony is what you taught me best,
its theory and its practical effects,
its gift in turning language on itself –
(Mark Antony might well have learned from you!).

Ironic in my turn, I now confess
the youth you labelled 'always courteous'
was that coarse wit who, in Assembly Hall,
would parody your 'Pirates of Penzance'
with lewd libretti, lavatorial.

Poetic too, I turned my back on school
a term before my time, to take a job
(without recourse to you as referee)
and thus confirmed pragmatic tendencies
yet gave the lie to your 'attendance' sop.

But that's all in the past; I've since returned
to your beloved Palgrave's Wordsworth, Keats,
discovered Larkin, Brownjohn, Harrison –
whose '*V*' I love as much as you would loathe –
and seen my own two volumes into print.

Should ever anybody ask me who
most influenced my work (though this assumes
the questioner had read me – and few do)
I'd own a major debt to you, and quote
this damning, treasured Testimonial.

Dear Mr. George, your irony still stings
as, carefully, I send new poems out
and, regularly, get them back again
from publishers whose pulse-rate must have peaked
were Typewriting the sole criterion.

BOLT FOR FREEDOM

for Matt Simpson – and all gatecrashers

'The purpose of poetry is to remind us
how difficult it is to remain just one person,
for our house is open, there are no keys to the door,
and invisible guests come in and out at will.'

Czeslaw Milosz

There now, it's done. I've bolted all my doors.
I've had it up to here being strung along
by poet puppeteers. Enough's enough.
I've raged against the dying light too long,
and cannot count how often drowned, not waved;

and what of all the times you've had me out
from daybreak drooling on that bloody bridge
at Westminster! I've got more urgent calls
to spend my days on: shopping; plants to pot;
and letters won't just write themselves, you know.

The peace you promised me on Innisfree
I failed to find. No, dropping bombs on Slough
was more my trip; cathartic, that, like when
you sent me with my aerosol to Leeds,
So, right, yer buggers, then, I thought, 'Cop this!'

My character's irrevocably changed –
I'm sure your lolly-stick did me no good!
And yet, fool that I am, I stayed to make
the cocoa for Old Wotsizname. But why,
so late in life, *the must of all those books?*

91

How mean, the stunt you pulled in '55,
and , knowing I don't smoke, you might have cleared
that saucerful of stubbed-out fags away
before you had me lie on Bleaney's bed –
and, anyway, those curtains drove me mad!

So far, I've humoured you. Not any more.
You're lousing up my biorhythmic flow –

– and if you think you'll get me, one more time,
to perch up in that fifth tier with my oar
and bust a gut to row your bloody tub
of ivory and peacocks all the way
from Ophir …
　　　　　　Boy! Have I got news for you!

RECAPTURE

I'd thought to free myself; that I should stay
out of your reach behind my bolted doors
and, there, to help in keeping you at bay
I concentrated on the household chores.

I spring-cleaned all the rooms and paid some bills –
the bathroom tiles have never shone so white.
My health improved, the doctor cut my pills
down to the knock-out two I take each night.

(If nicotine, booze, junk, sex, Tarot cards
and poetry are all addictive, I
had now one pressing need: renounce all bards!)
So, Wystan, Franceses, Johns, All – Goodbye!

Sometimes, I must admit, whilst dusting shelves
I'd feel the slightest tingle – nothing worse –
the one when suddenly we sense ourselves
observed – so skipped the shelf containing verse.

And during all this time, well shot of you,
released from all your hectoring I felt
so marvellously ME! I little knew
you'd stoop to hitting me below the belt.

Not quite below the belt – let's be precise,
more when my guard was down – but was it right
or gallant of you to exact your price
for one slip in my watchfulness, one night?

It happened when the children were asleep:
I'd just looked in, the way that parents will,
to see them safe and, whilst there, paused to peep
outside, between the curtains and the sill,

and that act brought back Bleaney's room once more –
one wayward thought, and liberty was lost!
But what recaptured me was what I saw:
the *moonlight lying on the grass like frost.*

The doors sprung wide – my dream of freedom ends
with, *on the highest pavement of the stair,*
the *wheelbarrow* on which *so much depends;*
that *silk hat on a Bradford millionaire.*

MR LARKIN

This was Mr. Larkin's bike. He rode
it all round Hull and Holderness, until
his need to scarper faster from the toad
egged him to motoring. And look, it still

bears scars and rust-pox down the near front fork
where he fell off, that night returning home
half-drunk on *Which* and washing sherry talk
from Warlock-Williams' do. On it he'd comb

the lanes of Patrington, Sunk Island, Paull,
in search of – what? An iffy tanner left
as conscience-geld in some church plate? Of all
that time torn off unused: those days bereft

of poems; nights starved of sex? Or did he look
for what he'd never found in booze and bars
nor teased out from the pages of a book;
something he'd left at home, perhaps? That vase?

It's dodgy ground, I know, to say these trips
away from cut-price crowds spelt more of gain
than loss, to claim he wrote from cycle clips
as profitably as he did by train.

But if he thought, death-suited, swerving east
back from some Lit-bore London interlude,
that here in Hull was where it mattered least
what foreign poets said; shivered, and viewed

'abroad' as inhospitable, cold, dark;
and slowing into Paragon he'd glow
with hope that not too far from Pearson Park
he'd find a new Parnassus, I don't know.

THIS BE THE CURSE

I fucked them up, my Mum and Dad;
I didn't mean to, but I did
by cropping up late, when they'd had
their seventh and, they'd thought, last kid.

But they fucked me up in my turn
by handing their libido down
and setting me on course to earn
repute as Randiest Buck In Town.

My life's one endless ding-a-ling –
What, me, complaining? I'm no fool –
until Mum's voice calls up to bring
me down from dreams, and late for school.

ROME IS SO BAD

Rome is so bad. Wartime, I thought it fine,
a place to come, see, conquer, then stay on.
So why did chaps like Hadrian take the line
forsaking lives of lust, and turn for fun
to humping stone from Solway to the Tyne?

Was it religion limited their scope?
Like when, a virgin squaddie, I found sex:
the Via Nuova, Carla – paid in soap
and fags – her bed beneath the crucifix,
Madonna watching from the wall. That pope.

THE AUTUMN OUTINGS

That autumn, I was quick getting away:
            only about
one-twenty on the rain-drenched Wednesday
I locked the premises and motored out,
all staff sent home, all workshop plant closed down,
all sense of any kind of business gone,
and not until I'd driven fifteen miles
along fast-flooding roads back into town,
past rival complexes just clinging on,
did rain let up and vision clear: those files

I'd never see again; that desk, the phone
            that shrilled all day
when first it was installed; not hear the moan
compressors made, be soothed by lathes, nor say

'Good morning George, alright?:' or 'Nice one, Bert',
the human touch, no more, not to distract
them too long from their work, but just enough
to let them see I cared, and not to hurt
old feelings as I tried to breast the fact
of cancelled orders, creditors turned rough.

The friendly bank soon bared its teeth – drew blood;
        and then that bane,
the Tax Man, claimed his pound. And so, the flood.
(Fine detail dims again as, too, the pain
recedes three autumns on; yet loss stays true.)
The rain comes vicious now – wipers full speed,
dipped headlights on, rear fogs – the journey seems
to lengthen every time I live it through,
involuntarily, as when the need
for sleep is scuppered by recurring dreams.

My crowd was breast-fed clichés, meal on meal:
        to pull its weight,
nose to the grindstone, shoulder to the wheel,
and, once it stepped inside the factory gate,
was wedded to its work; slapped all the time
by Newbolt's hand: *Play up, and play the game.*
Well, this sounds fine; but what about the bloke
who's anorexic, short-nosed, cannot climb
to reach the wheel, and never makes the team?
For him such wedding tales are guffs of smoke.

Again the morning paper hits the floor –
        banner headlined:
PIT CLOSURES SHOCK – and umpteen thousand more
are facing broken marriages to mines.
A few, lured by that bit-of-fresh, fool's gold,
pin hopes on boarding-houses, market stalls;
one man sits out his protest down the pit,
while lefties call for strikes with all the old
clenched-fist salutes, and aerosol the walls:
SCARGILL FOR KING and TARZAN IS A SHIT.

Their first few days of idleness will see
        in those it hits
undreamt-of traits in personality:
some will get by and others go to bits;
the strong become the weak, the weak make good
as quickly as it's said. Then, as the days
stack up to months or, as in my case, years,
high principles get trampled in the mud
where guile and self-survival point new ways
to quick back-pocket jobs, fiddles, and fears

of being caught. But fears will yield, in time,
        a sort of pride,
though not the social pride that saw men climb
from old-world swamps: a sense that one's defied
the odds, the system; finger-licked the crème,
nose-thumbed some top brass, bested those who made
the rules and all the running. What survives?
Of Us: too early yet to tell. Of Them:
'Indifferents and Incapables'; their trade
in UB40s and P45s.

In brass-lined boardrooms up and down the land
	deep in regret
a million more redundancies get planned,
while chairmen's hiked-up salaries are set,
and Urban Councils chase arrears in rents.
Wideboys, insider-dealers, some M.P.s
grow richer by a second home in Spain,
a custom-plated white Mercedes-Benz,
that new portfolio. True-blue disease.
The spores of loss, somewhere becoming gain.

October, 1992

POSTSCRIPT TO MY FATHER

'Über Sternen muss er wohnen'
		Friedrich Schiller, *'An die Freude'*

Those not-forgotten soured days, the booze-
blitzed nights, dawn absences – the man I knew
but mostly didn't. Dad, tonight I choose
to break with these and find a later you,

the one I took to golf, saw home again
drunk on the laughter of a fluked par-three,
and baited-up for, once on Hedon Drain –
work-knackered, dragging your redundancy –

that time you grassed a 2-ounce roach and caught
the smit, remember? Lately, those few days
snatched in maturity return – hard-bought,
the bill paid in advance. If there were ways

99

of reeling-in snagged lines to cast again
in new-found swims, could you or I resist?
Some unfished pool: who knows what specimen,
what sport, what joy! This time the catch not missed

like football in the park or Guy Fawkes Night,
the conkering we never got to share
or subtleties of keeping-up a kite ...
Those got away before. Dad, if I dared

believe you'd found an afterlife, I'd wish
– no, pray – this postscript reach you there above
tonight's brief stars: I know a stream, a fish
which, lured, hooked and landed, could be love.

AFTER THE PARADE

A HIGH HORIZON, 1927

First day at school – and aren't you back there now?
And isn't that her hand, its loosened hold
on yours now letting go: her smiled goodbye
that doesn't bring her face the shape it should?
And are you in a flag-stoned yard, with walls
a high horizon, playing back your yells,
scuffed ball and fag-cards? When that whistle blows
what is it goes from you? Simplicity?

They told you God was good, the Board Man bad;
that God could see you always, bad or good.
You didn't think to ask them where God lived
and never saw the Board Man, but believed –
or said you did. What was it spoiled the game
of all things bright and beautiful? Whose shame?

BEING THERE

Then, I was Fletcher Christian – never Bligh;
at other times, Ben Gunn (that toasted cheese!).
I'd dream ball-bearinged roller skates, new bikes
with Lauterwasser handlebars, toe-clips
and black bum-cutting saddles shoulder-high.
Soon it was girls, skirts hitched above the knees,
light-laced Hungarian blouses – summer hikes,
sequins of sweat, ear lobes and, always, lips.
I dreamed of good exam grades, wavy hair,
a uniform, demob, job, cash to spare
and winning for the kiddies at the fair.

Now, I have scary dreams and these recur –
like not to reach the loo in time; like where
I'm reading that I'm dead, and being there.

AN IDEAL COUPLE

They see us arm-in-arm or hand-in-hand
and smile benign good mornings as we pass;
we're such an ideal couple, so, they say,
our body language tells them. Well, OK,
no need to put them wise. But why should folk
assume that hand-in-hand or arm-in-arm
means we're a pair who don't *have words* or, worse,
don't throw a wobbler, dishcloth, hawked-up curse,
leave home – or threaten to, put on a hat,
then don't? Why must they shape us to their mould:
a blissful match, close-hitched yet hanging loose?
Hell's bells, no marriage should be sad as that!
Give us the sweet-and-sour, the hot-and-cold,
the knock-for-knock, the educated truce.

THE BIT-BAG

for Olive

Behind the cupboard door beneath the stairs,
where perished rubber macs hung stiff with fright,
her bit-bag gorged and fattened, week on week,
against the time when Mum would flood the floor
with yesterdays of velveteen, chenille,
green taffeta, shantung, that leather glove –
two digits gone for fingerstalls – grey spats,
in search of what she never seemed to find.

Times now I empty out and tell like beads
this bit-bag we've collected. Nothing's lost:
the diamond I first slipped you in the Grand,
our Crystal, Silver, Ruby, many jades.
Flawed gems, I cherish all of them, but most
your palsied smile I know the smile beyond.

FLU SURVIVOR

Pillow, and out;
a bender of a night –
the black suitcase
and the runaway car.

Grab, and hold on tight
if morning offers –
abandon the songbird
choked in its environs,

fling off the headband, wet
and shrinking fast,
stamp out the staging-camp,
the bent ration barons,

escape the sinking island
and the mocking gulls,
silence the shouts of the long dead
answering their echo,

cling fast to morning,
home, the suitcase
back on the wardrobe top
closing its lid.

THAT'S CHANNEL 4 NEWS

for Jon Snow

1. The Abacus

'Two, and a miniature' was my reply –
emboldened by the doctor's searing wit:
'You mean you've *three*?' – when I'd called in to tell
about the lump I hadn't known was there
until that TV news spot had me look
and feel, testicularly, in a way
I'd never done before. We laughed – his face
confirmed *he* meant it too – more likely I
just mimed him, dropped my pants and turned a bit
to face the light. His hands are warm, 'Mmmm, well,
for sure you've more here than the normal pair;
not certain what it is.' He takes a tuck
of scrotum, kneads it, lets it go, 'I'd say
don't worry – but we'll have a scan in case,
be on the safe side, eh? Up with your breeks.'
I've waited for the X-ray now four weeks –
that's almost ninety bathroom curtain-calls
at three a day, the abacus my balls.

2. Miscount

The giant panda in the waiting-bay's
no cheer to me; the teddy bear is blue
and lies face down; the woman opposite
is hyper-fidgety and sucks her gums –
I'm glad there are no mirrors here to show
myself to me. It echoes round the walls,

106

my name, and served up, supine, for the scan
I watch the radiographer who plays
a gelid mouse around, across and through
my wedding-tackle zone, till bit by bit
he's built the global picture. Now he comes
to what I've waited – seems like years – to know,
the count-up and condition of my balls:
just two, in fact, an almost normal man,
except there's this two-centimetre cyst –
plus one about 5-mill my fumblings missed.
The drive back home's a breeze, and every sign
along the road repeats 'Benign,' 'Benign!'

July/August 1995

HER GREEN

I'm watching for my wife, she's in her green
again today. Or fawn, with matching shoes.
Or was it blue? Shopping we always meet
just here for home. Or nearly always do.
Sometimes I've waited ages and she's been
the other end. It's politic I lose
our argument what side of just which street
we'd said. There goes another 22.
She'll be alright. I used to have a niece
drove buses. That a siren? Coming near –
or not? Hearing's half shot. I never know
which one's an ambulance and which police.
Her green... I'm sure. The one she bought last year.
After her fall. God, how the time goes slow.

ROTHBURY REVISITED

Five righthand turns, uphill and down again,
a clockwise whirl, to find this cul-de-sac
behind the flowering cherries, mountain ash
and cypress roosts – and just in time for tea
with home-baked scones and talk of how and when
we'd been this way before, what brought us back,
our almost fifty years gone in a flash,
how cul-de-sacs were not for you and me
and, after tortuous ups and downs we'd known
so recently, our need of calm to clear
the build-up of birdnesting in the head.
It's times like this when love has upped and thrown
more gold into the melting-pot, like here,
first time for months, we rumple just one bed.

CARROT CAKE

She greets me every week like family
around the back, her bolted kitchen door
a knuckle-crack of action blazoning
the moment I arrive – she knows my time,
my footfall down the path, can recognize
my outline through her cataracts. The door
lets out a stink of cats and locks me in
to sit and talk two hours over tea
in tannined cups her great-aunt Lucy left.
The cake she's baked, and I've declined, she'll wrap
for me to take... 'a treat for in the week.'
Back homeward through the park, the mallards know
my time, and as I leave, an argument
of sparrows comes to clear the path of crumbs.

GILFILLAN

Gilfillan would have loved to witness this
performance of his sons who've come to take
their final leave of him. He'd know they'll miss
his acid tongue and none will leave this wake
the worse for grief; that as they sit around
to eat his food and drink their own good health
each weaselling conversation will be drowned
obliquely by another, till his wealth
remains the only course for tongues and wine
to work on. How he'd relish this debate –
he having blown his stash at eightynine
and knowing that what's left of his estate
will bring them little but the blood's bequest:
to each the greed he sees in all the rest.

ULYSSES SMITH

'How dull it is to pause, to make an end,
To rust unburnish'd, not to shine in use!'
                                    Tennyson

Yes, that's his chair, and him asleep – his dream
perhaps the one in which he pans for gold
successfully along a mountain stream,
or if not that, could be he dreams the old
repeat of how he takes the trophy when
his chip-shot to the long eighteenth goes in.
The dullness, even rust, awaiting men
like him who're tossed into the offcut bin

with yesterday's steel pen and office stool
might mean a one-way ticket to the void
for lesser men than Smith, but he's no fool –
two fingers to the *gainfully employed*,
let Penny think he frets his time away –
Smith's chuckling in his dreams again today.

BREWER

Bruhière, Brugière, bruyère.
Sampling, sparging the grain,
here with the bitter hops
and the living yeasts of language,
oh, I could get drunk.

Here, *when the malt begins*
to get aboon the meal,
sitting with poets: *Skalds,*
Minnesingers, poet of the poor
and the uncrowned prince.

Here, words I could
soak in, *soft words*
that butter no parsnips,
words to conceal thoughts, words
that fill no bushel.

Could get stoned on the poetry
of Persian, Arabic; speaking
French to my friends,
Italian to my mistresses –
all of them, here.

Stewed, high, canned, smashed,
drunk as Chloe, blotto
on the birdsounds of English
singing and sibilant. Soused.
Oh, couldn't I just.

HOUSE GUEST

for Rosa, who felt a poem coming on

You sense it nearing; there's a hint of fear;
it waits outside your gate, its lion's nose
and human eyes surprise you and it could
possess you, make you feel a little less
the mistress of your stress-beleaguered niche
should you forget to lock up tight each night
or let it leap the fence to creep inside
your hallway, up the stairs to maul your dreams.

But pause a while; why should its coming cause
alarm? Would there be harm in offering
the beast a homely welcome? Not the least.
Well then, be brave, go meet it up the drive
and if you dare, give it the cosiest chair
in all your house. There – quiet as a mouse.

VIEW FROM HESSLE ROAD

for Jean Hartley

Old Bikeclips with the size 12 Oxfords wrote,
but eloquently, of *a cut-price crowd.*
I'm here to argue on a moral note
not that his choice of phrase be disallowed,
but that perhaps there's something to be learned
in asking why it was he wrote of them,
not they of him. Supposing that we turned
the *flat-faced trolley* round for once; what then?
Let's say we told those *grim* and *head-scarfed wives*
from *fishy-smelling streets* that they were owed
a swipe at Hull's late bard: 'Oozee?' perhaps
they'd gob out from *the side of their own lives,*
'We've never 'eard of 'im down 'Ezzle Road.
No, bollocks. Poetsarra… crowdacraps!'

OVER THE RAINBOW

I need to talk of wills and legacies,
ask would she like my books, and he my tools;
to know Gran's silver tray will not be sold
when I slip off the twig (a flippancy
I use to lessen their embarrassment).
They can't imagine why a Dad so fit
should even think about… they daren't say death
but *passing on…* and on my birthday, too!

112

They show me Florida and Disneyworld,
my grandchildren in Kodacolor smiles,
and whisk me to the pub, a bar-stool lunch,
four gins – or was it five – to buck me up
and then… *Oh, how time flies!*… they drop me off
back home, half-drunk, unlistened to – and leave.

DISPLACED PERSONS

D.P.s we called them, World War Two – a term
like Naafi, Amgot, Abca, kip and char
we used to fill the ennui between war
and demob – *hardly our concern, y'know:*
civilians, undisciplined, no firm
allegiance on the field of play, they mar
the whole damned shooting-match. And so our door
was shut on hordes of them.
                                    An hour ago
I surfaced from a T.V. doze, and in
their camp across my room were, staring out
half-pleading, half-accusing, thousands more.
I switched to 3… Old People's Homes.
                                    Now, in
a retake, there's my father, serving out
his time towards that comfiest chair; the door.

AFTER THE PARADE...

V-J Day, 15.08.1995

...the dustcart, fifty years of memory
of memories like laminates of paint
on seaside guardrails chipped away to show
what rusts beneath – or, put another way,
like sweets we sucked as kids, through every change
of colour to the central aniseed
we crushed between our teeth and knew again
the burped-up-baby tang of gripe-water.

We've sucked on this last half-a-century
of shadings from most vivid to more faint
relived experience, and still don't know
the peace we say we crave. No *Year*, no *Day*
lets us return to neatly rearrange
what's lost in war, obliterates our need
to rewrite scripts enacted way back when
we lacked the nous of mother, wife or daughter.

Four generations will have marched before
the dustcart's cleared the debris of my war.

AND SATURDAY IS CHRISTMAS
(NEW POEMS 1996 – 2010)

A TREE IN ST. ANDREW'S

*In memory of Thomas Amour Scott who died on 25th May 1996 aged 49
and for Jean*

1. The Wedding
– afternoon, 2nd May 1996

Their sunlit lounge,
dust motes, fresh
flowers and cards
on shelves, Lego
out of sight;
chased gold rings
chosen in haste,
a matching pair.
The registrar
with her book,
occasional husk
in her voice
and the gift
of a tear
in her eye
as she left
the houseful
of smiles
and a camera
whose film
came out
blank.

2. Mesothelioma

Those few days
eked out how –
not to die –
but to live
for the hour
where nothing
more mattered
but their love;
not the sun
or the moon
or the wind
through the night;
not their songs
or the letter
he didn't get
to write.

3. Shuttle

We learnt them
the hard way,
those three-and-half hours
holding two homes
to far sides
of counties,
by Malton and Thirsk,
via Ainderby Quernhow
with the seething A1
in between.

Ten times
or a dozen
we stopped off
at Birtley
for petrol.

And homeward
we'd fastlane
to the Bank-climb
at Sutton
where we'd pull in
for coffee
and wind down
side-windows
to bait-up
the bonnet
with breadcrumbs
for finches
which shuttled
the carpark
between us
and their young.

4. Perspective

After he'd died
his kindly nurse
and the doctor
stayed on

by the body
and talked
with his widow
about what

to do next
and of how
it would be…
till the boy

with a pig
he was making
of blue felt
and cottonballs

bubbled in
to ask how
he should finish
the stitching

and she knew
this was just
how it always
would be.

5. Night

When the carers
had left
came the policeman,
his official report –

more important
than grief –
made Tom's body
no longer his own

nor yet Jean's
but the State's.
Dark-suited shapes
then slalomed her man

around landings
down stairs and away
through the night
she had begged

they might share
one last time
in their room
until dawn.

When they'd gone
all the lights
in the house
were left on.

6. How It Was

While
he was dying
she was
his wife:
nursing,
feeding him,
strong.

After
he'd died
she was
our daughter:
cursing;
needing us;
frail.

7. Evening

Leaving her home
for the Chapel
of Repose
the last time
she'd see him

she waved
to her children
at play
with their friends
in the drive.

"Where're you off?",
called her son.
"To see Tom",
she replied.
"Can I come?",

asked the lad.
His wise sister's
"You can't want
to go see
a dead body?"

brought a shout
from the gang.,
whose interest
in skateboards
swerved off course,

"Yeah, can *we*?".
Did a smile rouge her cheeks
as I drove
her away?

   8. Pachelbel's Canon

When the music
had stopped
she left
his coffin

behind curtains.
She'd have taken
the ashes next day
had they let her

to the woodland,
but the man
said he needed
more time

not in respect
for the dead
but for reasons
of cooling.

9. Acer Platanoides

Without priest or prayerbook
the maple was planted;
no trite protestations or hymns:
just the words of his widow,
some friendly farewells,
a reading of Larkin's *The Trees*.

Now, returning alone
with a watering-can
to the tree
where his ashes are laid,
she talks to him, softly
again, of small things:

the currants a rabbit's left
ringing his stone,
a pheasant's harsh call
from the fringe-grass,
then she paints him the mural
she finished this week,
talks of the children at school.

If he hears of the tremors
of panic, self-doubt,
or her tears at odd times
through each day, who's to know?
But the wind will speak out
of the rage that she hurls
in its face as she leaves.

Hexham, 1996

SANTOS TO SANTA CRUZ DELLA SIERRA

with Lisa St. Aubin de Terán

Soon after changing trains I must have slept;
Lisa was chatting to a man in shades
she'd met in São Paulo where the sun
backlit the arsehole of the world. We'd swept
away from Luz, from crack cocaine, dawn raids,
bent cops, cheap lives, the rule of knife and gun.
I couldn't quite make out their Portuguese
with Villa-Lobos in the background, so
I'd nodded off. The motion of the train?
The heat, her voice, the music? All of these?
I blinked through Campo Grande, its plateau
of sugar-men, heard Lisa's voice again,
crashed out past San José, missed Santa Cruz
completely. Woke to Yorkshire's local news:
the after-Christmas snows, a car-crash scene,
my wife's "A drop more plonk? The dustman's been".

'Great Railway Journeys', BBC 2 TV ® 02.01.1997

125

A NOVICE STACKER TALKS HERSELF TO SLEEP

for The Staff of Bridlington Library on its 60th anniversary

Applied Mathematics, Zionism, Jung
Spike Milligan, Dirk Bogarde, Mao Tse Tung,
Kes, Kingsley Amis, Dickens, Graham Greene,
Maeve Binchy, Secret Lives, The Time Machine,
The Cruel Sea, A Guide To London Parks,
Karate, Jeffrey Archer (Yuk!), Karl Marx,
Jack Kerouac, The Grapes Of Wrath, Ben Hur,
Disraeli, Wisden, Colditz, Rupert Bear,
Victoria Glendinning, Deng Xiaoping,
From Jazz To Bebop Via Blues And Swing,
Bob Dylan, Dylan Thomas, Thomas Moore,
Who's Who, Mein Kampf, Exploring Ecuador,
The Naked Ape, Jurassic Park, D Day,
The A to Z of ...A to Z of ...A...

1997

FUNNY OLD WORLD

She made a rare old joke of it for me
and thousands more, that upstart, grocer's lass.
Not of the world completely, but of dreams
like how for some of us the cards might be
more favourably dealt. Nor should it pass
unchronicled that of the ice-blue schemes
she gave her name to, few if any were
to benefit her gender, lift the girls,
born-losers near the bottom of the heap,
a peg or two. But me, I feel for her
a porcine glow, for casting me the pearls
of private ownership – and on the cheap!
I made a bomb, a killing some might say,
in repossessions, shares and, by the way,
laughed off old dreams. Those losers? *Their* affair!
What, me and Maggie Roberts, we should care?

THE WORLD AT EIGHT

for A.M.R-M

For him, the world is Lego, mountain bikes,
a working world of crane jibs, traverse rings,
derailleur gears and cantilever brakes –
which might suggest that Alec only likes
mechanically oriented things
in life. Not so; too simple, that. He makes
the cuddliest of pigs you've ever known
from coloured felt – blunt snouts and button eyes –
and turns his hand to other, gentler arts
like giving Gran a kiss when they're alone
at story time – she thrills to the surprise!
Not short on literary flair, in parts,
he uses words like 'gullible', and while
he may write 'nice' as 'nise' he shows great style
with dinosaurs, can spell – and this takes nerve –
'velociraptor' perfectly. There's verve!

*Velociraptor: a small carnivorous dinosaur of the Cretaceous period
having a single long curved claw on each hind foot.*
– OED

THE WORLD AT TWELVE

for K.H.R-M

I peeped inside your room to see the wall
where Mum's subaqua mural crowns her long
devotion to the practice of fine arts,
and, yes! you're into Spice Girls now, with all
the actions, all the words of every song!
Encyclopedic knowledge of The Charts
is *de rigueur* and so, from just above
your bed the five smile down – top of the pops
with Boyzone. Smash Hits ring the VDU
that guards your desk. 'Don't Stop Looking For Love',
you sing; palazzo pants, peep-belly-tops
and platform shoes, your dream. Dreams can come true
so, Katy-Love, although your heart may ache
at times, be sure, when life's a piece of cake
you taste it to the full, don't miss one crumb.
Hold to your dreams, the best is yet to come.

A WIND GETTING UP

'Non sono mai stato certo di essere al mondo'
                    Eugenio Montale, *Zenia 11.*

Me too. And that chap Muggeridge once swore
he'd never felt entirely at home
in this world – but with him I never knew
which of his many party-hats he wore:
philosopher or roué, garden-gnome
or sage. Supposing that his claim was true,
I wonder if he'd thought himself unique
as I had when in – was that youth? – I found
or thought I'd found that I was out of sync
with current norms but didn't choose to speak
about what seemed unmacho and to sound
alarm bells like "What will the neighbours think?".
Now in old age, I ask which friend could claim,
which neighbour swear, he'd never felt the same?

Took time to feel at home, and now I hear
the breeze beyond the door, I'm comfy here.

KINDERWELT

When Gerda Bluhm was getting on for nine
and Myra not yet two, a bond was sealed
as sometimes happens in a family where
an elder daughter finds herself in line
to play the rôle of mother and to yield
to vulnerable siblings all the care
an absent parent might. So, Gerda led,
and Myra absorbed all her idol taught
by sheer example, higher intellect,
a love that grew. They neither of them wed.
They're in their eighties now and time has caught
at Gerda's hem. Sometimes, she can't connect.
The care-nurse comes, a youngster full of praise
for Gerda's answers to her "little quiz",
"That's good! Now spell 'world' backwards." Myra says,
but softly, "Backwards, *stimmt*, that's how it is."

MIST

Thought is reluctant today,
tentative for what we know
but cannot clearly see.
The low sky defies description,
telling only of absence;
the blank page its facsimile.

Not a bird sings or comes
to the sill where we sit
held in our own keeping.
Just now, I glimpsed her face
as it was, in your glance,
but dared not look again.

Outside, mist gathers its wrap
closer, becomes introvert.
We, too, keep our silences,
missing her – but unable to share
memories clearer than the day –
and all the draughts she made.

And there'll be more such days,
dumb, listless, without view,
before wind and rain return
perspective, when necklets of mist
hang from the trellis, break,
fall, and stain an empty page.

SHORT STRAW

They're showing it again, for goodness sake!
I watched it last week, and a month ago,
in fact it's been repeated year on year,
this one, or 'Casablanca' –I mistake
the Bogey film for 'Brief Encounter'. So,
what happens is, because new films are dear,
three schedulers draw straws to see whose can
to dig up from the vaults while heavies keep
watch where the D.G's magic mushrooms grow.

I e-mailed 'Points of View', asked for a ban
on these old weepies, though in truth I sleep
equally well through each and, as they know,
to those who've shunned the grave as long as me,
newborn, or disinterred, TV comes free.

But though my plea for change was not in vain
I'm now zapped off, catnapping by a plain
dumb screen, afraid to switch it on again
and catch my death through 'Singing in the Rain'.

PRE-OP

"I'm in the their bloody *charpoy* with my chest,
not that down there.", he waves away her cup.
"Hush, Dad", she takes his hand, "Just try to rest".
But once he's spurred, the old man can't shut up,
"Those quacks've got their bumf mixed, stupid berks,
I only leak a bit – just hold your rein –
it's those lot came in with their waterworks,
the ones with plastic bags and tubes to drain
inside their 'jama legs…" – She knows too well
his problem, stubborn sod, didn't she call
to do him daily, carry home the smell
of cavalry, his Aldershot, Bengal –
"…they'll fit no bloody *ganga-pouch* to me –
I'll stand and do it proper when *I* pee!".

THE MUSIC-MAN

If, when they'd asked me for my date of birth,
I'd said the same day that they'd locked away
the music-man insane, who'd tasted earth
in France and breathed-in German toxic spray
for England and King George's-shilling war,
would they have interrupted, "Say no more!"?

And had I dared expound: the time of Bloom
as Joyce's *Ulysses*, the year that saw
The Waste Land, Tutankhamen's tomb;
the day and month The System slammed the door
on freedom for the music-man, how few
could date it twentyeight-nine-twentytwo?

But fifteen years' 'safe-keeping' failed to stall
his music's flow from brain to score, or dim
a poet's view of Brimscombe pines, the fall
of rain on Cotswold hills. Though, not for him
recitals of his songs, his poems read:
when plaudits came, the music-man was dead.

Among his lines that shame us, here are two –
it hurts to read them but I must, and do
grieve for the music-man denied his need –
Prussians of England, weep for him, and read:

"They have left me little indeed, how shall I best keep
memory from sliding content down to drugged sleep?"

                           – Ivor Gurney

LADY OF THE TOWN

She'll bone you in a mall or city street –
quite likely there'll be two, some yards apart
but if you see her first you'll look away
and hurry by, especially if your wife
has lugged you shopping and you've neither time
nor fancy for her propositioning.

Sometimes, alone, I'll loiter on her beat –
unwittingly, of course. She'll up and start
her spiel on me: how I could make her day…
and would I like…OK? Well, for my life
I can't say no to girls. Alright then, I'm
your man. It's over soon. She'll do her thing
a few more times then be back home by six,
her clipboard filled and worth its weight in ticks.

A POETRY ANORAK RECALLS SOME HOUSE
GUESTS

John Masefield, Ivor Gurney, Douglas Dunn,
Ruth Fainlight, Elaine Feinstein, Yeats, Thom Gunn –
(he talked at length on motorbikes, and birds;
I loved him for the thunder in his words).

George Orwell, Henry Reed, Gavin Bantock,
Joyce, Shelley, Isherwood, Hilaire Belloc –
(soon tired of him, more quickly of his rhyme;
banged on about his money all the time).

The Thomas clan: Edward, R.S, Dylan,
Charles Causley, Keats, Pamela Gillilan,
Matt Simpson, Robert Southey, Rupert Brooke,
(when Auden came, I tried hard not to look
at tramlines on his face; the poems have stood).

Charles Kingsley, Manley Hopkins, Thomas Hood,
Rossetti (both of them), the Brownings, Burns,
Lord Byron, Larkin, Eliot – Thomas Stearns –
(that *Waste Land*, Notes and all – above my head;
I wept beside his garden urn instead).

Anonymous (he sneaked in) Charlotte Mew,
three brace of Johns (on leave from Peterloo).
Keith Douglas, Hughes, Ken Smith, Patricia Beer,
Charles Lamb, Gray, Goldsmith, Shakespeare…

Apologies for absence? One I'd cull:
that horny git, who had it big to pull
nice Ganges girls; wife phoned – train was too full!
(my bet she'd shrunk him, in the tide off Hull).

TURKEY AND TINSEL

For pensioners, a cheapo: Five-Day Break.
Pretending, in November, that today
is Christmas Eve, we board the coach to take
us down to Eastbourne where, the brochures say,
we'll have a *Christmas as it used to be.*
Fat chance! Folk at the fag-end of their lives,
all spectacles and hearing-aids and pee –
or wanting to. Some eating from their knives
and putting others off, their clacking teeth
like castanets from Costa Brava days.
And pushy! Some of them are quite beneath
contempt. Him, with his rude and grabbing ways
we've soon got taped: all cummerbund and crap.
We beat him to the bar – first drink is free,
a squabble starts, we almost have a scrap.
Adeste! Christmas as it used to be.

COUNTING THE CARDS

'The Infant Saviour', 1493
by Albrecht Dürer; Launceston; Gordale Scar;
from 'Chagford through the Ages' – Wendy Mee;
Spain – Barcelona. Greetings from afar

and not so far – The Minster, Beverley
just down the road from here. Titbits of news.
Kowloon; Porthcawl; thatched roofs at Shottery;
more of the same in Cockington; six views

from you-know-where in Greece; Matisse; a Bosch;
'All Greek' by Pauline – vibrant, oil on board;
a bureau by Charles Rennie Mackintosh;
two Canalettos adding to the hoard.

My earliest is postmarked '92,
by Wessily Kandinsky, called 'Blue Sky –
a detail'. *Shoestring* Poem Cards; a few
more gems of art to tease and hold the eye;

Japan – Atami Hot Springs, '94;
the wilderness of St. Columba, Tas.;
Aegina once again – blue-painted door
in front of which a sharp-eyed snapper has

immortalized three kittens as they play.
Each valued then, all priceless to this day,
I've totted up, as keen curators do,
repeating "Bestest, John' times eightytwo!

DRIFTWOOD

We came with our hopes
to walk by the Swale
in a warming sun;
instead we leaned
on the nithering wind
and prised our way upstream,
tears uncontrollable
like words we used to hurt.

At Gunnerside we turned
rucksacks to the wind,
sat on the low wall
with flasks of coffee, biscuits
and oblique expectancies
while the softwater beck
bucked and shied away
from our brittleness of words.

A flitting of April snow,
like the feathered grey
of our bundled letters
she'd burned last autumn
with the orchard leaves,
and we walked, arms linked –
old habit as yet unbroken –
back to our weekend-let.

She prepared soup and croûtons
I collected the debris
of a winter's storm,
the river's driftwood,
to kindle fire on a cold hearth;
the syllables of smoke mocked
phrases of reconciliation
and were as quickly gone.

ON HIS SILENCE

for John Alderton & Pauline Collins

When I reflect on how my light yet glows –
although more dimly now, as years gone by
recalled – and so few poems written, I
still find iambic thought outsings my prose,

so why don't I catch poems while I can
conduct their rhythms falling on the page;
not make excuses: tiredness, old-age?
This is the poet manqué, not the man

fulfilled. But, hey! How mean of you that day
you phoned, to lure me with how John would lie
reciting Milton's *Blindness*, through a night

he couldn't sleep. I've sussed your bait! No way
you'll get me sitting down for one more try
to score a sonnet!
               Damn you both…
                       I might…

ROOTS

What is it we are holding to in age
that sets us reaching back to ancestry,
our social background, genealogy;
why has the family-tree become the rage?

For sure, when we were young we'd never look
behind; deep into work, lust, love, then kids.
Why now, so late, the need to force locked lids,
pierce privacies, unearth the close-kept book?

I'm sweating in the garden as I think
these thoughts, to oust this tree-stump, foot on fork
with all my nine-stone thrusting down the tines

and prising-up the roots to break their link
with all they've clung to. When it's done I'll walk
away, bathe, take this photo, probe these lines.

BEHIND THE LINES

Manor House Surgery, Bridlington

The waiting room is full
of sounds I hear encrypted
through the ears' stud walls.
I need my volume wheels
up high, so can't screen out
the dross of other patients'
Esperanto through a crush
of phonecallsdoorbangs
and the Johnny-get-your-gun
of small-arms fire, sporadic
from Children's Corner.
Booked in, attentively I blend –
at least pretend I do –
into the daily norm.
Time drags its muffled feet.

Then, when I've dropped my guard,
I'm rumbled. My number's up.
Alien in their land,
no *Ausweis* and without
the agent's cop-out happy-pill,
interrogation starts.
No need of blindfold –
they know that I can't read
the *Geheimestaatspolizei*
computer screen display
which bids me Happy Birthday

and prints my codename bold
as 'White Coat Hypertension' –
a sympathetic nurse told me
in English, loud and clear.

I've been this way before
and learnt by heart the drill:
that when they let me out
the codename stays behind
and I shall bluff my way
through *sotto voce* days
of almost-heard repeats
of nearly-heard repeats
in a strange soft-focus town,
read lips as best I can
and nod – sometimes correctly,
a foreign parachutist
lost behind enemy lines.
Survival pack: to learn
the one way out is through.

Stevie Smith is on record as having said that being alive was "like living in
enemy territory". The deaf and sight-impaired might well agree.

DOMESTIC SCIENCE

To push the vacuum cleaner round and curse
the pains of age, you'd never think that it
is useful when you're contemplating verse,

yet this can be a good time to rehearse
strict rhyme schemes – though I'd much prefer to sit,
to ride the vacuum cleaner round and curse.

Light exercise is fine, age shouldn't nurse
its ailments; effort, if it hurts a bit,
is needful when you're excavating verse.

Escape from pain can drive folk to immerse
themselves in art; I've hit on my gambit:
to coax the vacuum cleaner round and curse

and hope some muse, unlike a Shylock's purse,
will open readily, whose nous or wit
is helpful when you're incubating verse.

At eighty-eight, with old guests faring worse
or not at all, I gratefully submit:
to shift the vacuum cleaner round and curse
is fruitful when you're improvising verse.

> Also attributed to Stevie Smith:
> "My best poems come when I'm Hoovering the carpet."

LEYLANDIISAURUS RADIX

Leylandiisaurus Radix – there's a name
for you! The first part gives away the clue,
the last its root – a startled old man's game
I played in tagging what's now here to view
although it lay in darkness, quite unseen
for almost all its time, until that day
the loggers loosed their snarling chainsaws, keen
to slip the leash and savage – better say
to kill – our cypress. Blooded then, they'd left.
I dug, coaxed, tugged, until a final heft
won me a carcass, then I scrubbed and dressed
the bones, tinkered and tweaked for weeks, my quest
some curio, but never in my mind
this sonnet to a prehistoric find!

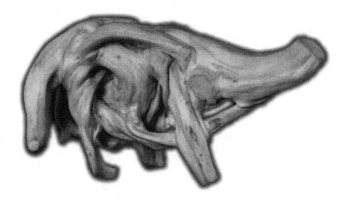

RED ADMIRAL

Should I prefer you to the fecund White
whose offspring worked my brassicas to lace
last year? You bet your life! But am I right
to welcome you so eagerly, to race
indoors and bring my camera to catch
your flashy Batman act, to freeze your frail
antennae in this moment where they'd match
the dawn-lit dewdrops on a spider trail?

Of course! Though, wait – let's be more circumspect
on why such vaudeville as yours should set
you higher up the scale of my respect
than dancing Whites whose drunken pirouette
also enriches me. Ah, now I'm loath
to differentiate. I need you both.

ENGLISH AND THE F-WORD

White fleet of plastic table-tops
with swab-down whorls, and quoits where cups
have jettisoned their overload;
no quay in sight, no ships to ride
the swell; the sea's two streets away.
Long-distance coaches stop close by
this 'Quayside Diner' where I wait
until the thirteen-fortyeight
for Hull arrives. "Mushrooms on toast"
a waitress bawls – an arm is raised;
"Double French fries" next out, and then
"Full English", "Number twenty nine".

Most tables have been spoken for.
I find one over by the far
loo door, ask "May I join you here?",
sit down, shunned by the hand-held pair
of bacon butties opposite.
I rest the mug of hot chocolate,
take out my pad and pen to write
these couplets, served up on a plate:
How wolfishly some English eat –
forgive me if I'm indiscreet –
back home in Germany we *essen*;
our dogs, short on decorum, *fressen*.

GLOSS ON THREE GUESTS

for Carol

1. from *January* by Frances Horovitz

A sealed stillness
— only the stream moves,
tremor and furl of water
under dead leaves.

Between the waking mind
and another dream, my hand,
questioning, again I find
a sealed stillness,

a cold bed, your love-lie.
Frozen now, the copse
across the way and I
— only the stream moves,

heedless, through fresh snow.
Friends tell me I'll warm,
thrill again, when Spring's flow,
tremor and furl of water

excite the rhythmic blood
to dance away your shadow,
let spent love lie in the wood
under dead leaves.

2. from *Masha* by Yevgeny Yevtushenko
                          translated by Lawrence Ferlinghetti
                          with Anthony Kahn

A girl goes along the seashore
blushing and shy
a tide rising in her
a woman rising in her

I ask the carefree surf could this be
my Masha, slender limbed, heel-and-toeing
the years away, when I watch how
a girl goes along the seashore

blooming with each brash wavelet's kiss
at her feet, until she turns, returns, answering
not yes or no, nearing me now,
blushing and shy

sensing my gaze. She is dating me now
earlier even than my father. I smile
a grandson's smile at her flowering, knowing
a tide rising in her,

its rollers, unstoppable, subsuming the strand
between our thoughts. Her smile perhaps
says perhaps. I turn away. I dare not see
a woman rising in her.

3. *The Return* by R.S.Thomas

What more to say? *Coming home was to that:*
Same silent God; unanswered cris de cour.
But there by the casement windows, from where
The white house in the cool grass could be seen
At times to gaze back, his succour, the seat
In part-sunlight, its cushions plumped-up neat
Membraned with shadows; the bright stretch of blue
Lleyn evening air that drew the poet's eye
Across the glebe to where he knew the sigh
Of stream that was its looking-glass below;

And smoke growing above the roof at dusk
When fire was lit and the black kettle whined
Dispersed, as wailing wind called back his mind
To a tall tree among whose boughs the storm
Had keened all through that day he'd prayed beside
Iago's rancid bed. As Prytherch died
The first stars renewed their theme: indifference –
Yet, curious now to see God's hurtful wrongs
Inspire a priest's return to poems, his songs
Of love, *of time and death and a man's vows.*

ROSIE

It's been so quiet, God, again today.
Now yesterday was different from the start:
the postman called – he couldn't make them hear
nextdoor. I took the parcel round backway
and nattered on their kitchen step best part
of half an hour. First chat we've had this year.
It did me good, Lord. Must've done because
I'd whipped my gladrags on and trundled off
to Tesco with my wheeliebag by ten!
Diane was on the checkout – full of sauce
as usual. We had a laugh. Real toff,
she is. So kind. Reminded me again
of Rosie: young, such zest for life, You know,
before that car... It's nineteen years ago
next week. Oh, where were You that day, God? Eh?
I ask you every night. You never say.

BIRTH OF A GREAT-GRANDDAUGHTER, 15.11.2009

Elyse Rose, Hi! (You're not yet half a day
into this high-tech world and here you are,
sharp, on our cellphone screen. What does this say
might shape your nursery days to come?) *Hurrah
for Mum – three times hurrah for you!* (We're pleased
you're here – by microchip and satellite!
But if you should skip baby-talk, be eased
straight into technospeak, the megabyte
your rusk with pixels as you teethe, and prove
life could be good at such a breakneck rate
slow down, sometimes, down to the speed of love
sent through the post, or phoned, or in your great-
grandparents' thick-thumbed, amateurish way)
we text, with l o l, this m s j.

PARLIAMENT WEBSITE, 18.06.2009

Today we have shaming of prats. Yesterday
we had bent accounting. And tomorrow morning
we shall have what they say after outing. But today,
today we have shaming of prats. The press corps
listens for howlers in all of the schoolboy excuses
       and today we have shaming of prats.

This is the Lower House Member, and this
is the Upper House Member whose use you will see
seldom if ever at all. And this is the honest Member
which in their case we have not got. Chisellers
cry over their chequebooks, returning a million or two,
       which in our case we have not got.

This is the silted moat, which is always cleaned
using contractors; the owner does not want to see
anyone dirtying their fingers; he can miss it quite easy
if he has an expense chit and cheek. The smart son
of woolsack has chutzpah in spades; no-one will see
       him dirtying his fingers.

And this you can see is the island. The purpose of this
is to keep predators from prey. Scared ducks make for it
rapidly backwards and forwards; they call this
closing the ranks. And rapidly backwards and forwards
leaders and whips are conferring and cooking up scripts:
       they call it closing the ranks.

They call it closing the ranks: it is perfectly easy
if you have the right motto or accent, wear the blazer
or tie, use the handshake. And the point of balance,
which in their case they have not got, has been lost
not on one of The Ten, but in forgetting The Eleventh,
      so today we have shaming of prats.

UPON WESTMINSTER BRIDGE

the rewrite, 2009

Fair as Westminster views might once have been,
By decadence we now see tarnished glitz,
Majesty's gone and scoundrels, as befits,
Wear shame where Wordsworth's *mighty heart* was seen.
Bare now for him to hate, each crude, obscene
Lie, replicated in fictitious flits,
Sky-high repair claims, freebies at the Ritz.
Air-brushed for years, the scam's become routine;
Steep bills abound whose fraudsters claim a mole-
Hill has been mountainized!
                    No matter how
Deep cankerectomy must cut, the hole
Will fill again. Would Wordsworth's wrath allow
Asleep into his poem? No, his soul
Still touched, would wake him for the rewrite now.

154

NOSEJOB

1. The Consultant

is a man
in a suit
and a hurry,
a time zone
adrift,
who is curt –
basal cell
carcinoma,
needs a flap,
leaves a scar –
He sketches
a nose,
left profile,
adds an S-bend,
closes my file
and jets off
in his search
for the missing
meridian.

2. The Nurse

is savvy, with it, can do
impossible things, tying strings
up the back of my smock.
She gives me blue shower-caps,
pulls them over my shoes

and snow-walks me through
to a winter-bright room
where she helps in my climb
to the frost-white plateau
of a bleak ironing-board,
then positions my head,
tissues sweat from my face.
Exchanging my specs for cool masks
under the Cyclopean stare
of the harsh theatre lamp
she turns day into night
and is gone.

3. The Surgeon

is a woman I soon get to know
I can trust, right after she says
this is the worst part, painful
at first but it's brief, tattooing
a circuit of locals on my sterilized nose.
She sounds young; her assistant does, too.
They haven't been a double-act long
but before the Cyclops gets killed
the pace of their patter will be proved.
Their voices blend closer as I metamorphose
from bit part to audience-of-one:

incision, swab, suction, specimen, more swabs,
hook on it, and *five-o-monochrome* punctuate
the duologue leached through my wraps
...wretched back-boiler exchange of contracts
hoarding clothes never worn with wardrobes

full in the attic woodworm saved hundreds
of pounds on treatment did all of it
himself a Sindy doll and My Little Pony
when that hated Crown Derby his mother left
has gone charity car-boot eBay who cares
it goes or I said on a glorious holiday
at Folkestone in Majorca he was glad I moved
in with him three years ago talk about cold
didn't last à la carte was too pricey
a béchamel sauce would have made such
a nice Italian or Chinese for me Indian
is too hot but the sea there is crystal
three grand was a bargain for evening wear
smart-casual with eye-level oven and grill
we'll do the other skin cancer next
if she's ready to come through yes alright
so how old are you now…

…there then that's you finished young man
you've done very well let's slip these wraps off
tidy you up rise slowly I'll help that's good
who's a pretty boy then keep the dressings
clean and dry for a week try not to bend down
best leave your glasses off for now take care…

4. The Theatre Assistant

is thirty.

ROLE-PLAY

When Larkin mooted *days are where we live*
he asked me – if a boss does ask – to give
some thought to this, re-build my bungalow
in temporal terms. Promotion-bent, a no
would spell finito Joe, so I agreed
to see where Sir's crackpot idea might lead.
In seconds I had footings firmly set;
in minutes, dampcourse laid, but how to get
the hours to bond together weathertight?
My friendly DIY books put me right.

But then I flipped, thought sod your sand and lime
and asked did all librarians spend time
in setting dickheads scratching for a rhyme.
He didn't answer. Miffed, he hatched his plan
to send me up for good. And thus began
my life as Arnold, and his 'Self's the Man'.

QED

I might have thrived on novels, like my friend
Sir Kingsley Whodidnicely, but I end
holed up near Hull, a writer much misread –
a crassness that persists though I'm long dead:
why should, say, lines about a coastal shelf
suggest a mean and miserable self?
Can't the fools twig when poetry's tongue-in-cheek,
not about me or mine, but more oblique
to fox the man I might have been, the chap –
or woman maybe – spouting arrant crap?
It's what and how, but not who writes the stuff,
that hold the reader rapt – they're quite enough.
The thought that spawned a poem was my own;
the poem isn't me, it stands alone
and should. Let critics flense us to the bone:
like love, the poem survives, as has been shown.

LETTER TO EDITH SÖDERGRAN

Dearest, is what you wrote quite fair:
my love was darkening your star?
Its meaning isn't very clear –

if darken doubles for eclipse
in astral terms, would this perhaps
describe a love that overtops

your own for me? Couldn't you say
it straight, my dear, rather than toy
with metaphor? But Liebschen, why

this thing about our hands? I missed
the point, bewildered, where you stressed
your hand was longing; my hand, lust!

Is there some nuance being lost
in my translation? I'd suggest
that lust is longing; longing, lust.

Then should my lust be deemed a fault
when only part of what I felt
for you? Edith, I take no guilt

from what I'd never thought a sin;
only regret, each evening, when
your hand is not at home in mine.

I'll miss you, Schatz, of course I shall –
there'll be no other love could fill
the void you leave. I wish you well.

FORLIMPÓPOLI

Somewhere, subliminal, in a gap
of gunfire: *non ti scordar di me.*
And no, I can't forget, nor would
if I could, December at Forlimpópoli.
A thousand times I've smelt again
mud, pungent as a tanner's bath,
kneaded by Sherman tanks with names
from home, Cheltenham, Chippenham,
we leaguered by those shellpocked walls.
The farmer's wife who might have been
himself but twice the man, watching,
waiting our help to raise the oak tun
buried under cold earth in the barn
where last night *Tedeschi* had slept;
her *Grazie a Dio* for the still sweet smell
of seedcorn casked for winter sowing
in the fields we liberated, re-occupied.
The sad, sad eyes, reproachful,
of a white ox in the stall, his flank
pulsing blackening blood, the rude
intrusion of impartial shrapnel.
How we left, muddling northward –
Ravenna, Tarvisio, Molzbichl –
our war, no longer her concern.
Natale, Weihnachten, Christmas,
and her one *bue bianco* limping
the sodden plough at Forlimpópoli.

LA GIOIOSA ET AMOROSA
PINOT GRIGIO BLUSH

La Gioiosa et Amorosa derives from a 14th century poet's description of the region of Italy near Treviso known as 'Marca Trevigiana'. It describes the area's joyful lifestyle and love of good wines.

Treviso, yes, I knew her briefly once,
not closely, but to pass the time of day
and common courtesies as, too, I knew
Tarvisio, her northern border kin;
but those were hardly joyous times for her,
with friendliness and loving put on hold.

Yes, I remember, am reminded, when,
with twenty thousand *Buona Seras* gone
to history, this bottle's label speaks
for one whose joyous visit brought us love,
whose going was too soon but kindly left
this blush of wine, a book of verse, and now...

INNOCENCE, 1960

Maincrop potato haulms are flowering now,
delicate mauves and yellows, innocent,
content within themselves, unquestioning,
indifferent to precision of their rows
in banked-up, frost-fined tilth his careful hands
have coaxed with hoe and rake; such artistry.

Last year I saw him double-dig this plot;
the youngster, not yet old enough for school,
I heard come up the path to ask him "What
are you doing, Grandad?" and be thrown
"Nothing to do with you." Then pressing, "Why

is it nothing to do with me, Grandad?".
"Because it isn't nothing to do with you."
The spade thrust deep again, sliced earth
clean as a butcher's cleaver severs chops.
Perplexed, the lad withdrew within himself

to find a wonderworld elsewhere. I held
my silence, stayed my own side of the fence
feeling the autumn chill, hearing the slape
and slap of spade and soil, of each cut clod
exposed to face a polystyrene sky.

Maincrop potato haulms are flowering now,
delicate mauves and yellows, innocent,
free from complicity. They share no shame.

EXPERIENCE, 2010

A July morning, humid, overcast,
brings me to Hull again, first time in years –
some notion of revisiting my past
now there's so much of it, confirms my fears

of change and alienation. Should have guessed
how takeovers and makeovers would kill
so many landmarks, camouflage the rest;
foolish to think the city could stand still

whilst I moved on.
                    A passing gust of gowns
declares I've chanced on Graduation Day –
a mix of mortarboards leaves other towns
by train for Paragon, then makes its way

towards Victoria Square, the City Hall
its destination, fussed along by proud
mothers in summer frocks, some dads, and all
to swell the made-it, so-far-so-good crowd.

The Ferens is my goal. Here in the cool
faintly disturbing, viewer-friendly air
I make for Edgar Bundy's oil, *Night School*
uneasy, as when first I stood to stare.

Though scarring of the macula impedes
my vision now, I know the young man's look
of mild bewilderment; the chart he reads
is less distinct, as also is his book

which lies unopened. Has the candlelight
dimmed too? Those older men, behind, who pore
over set literature late into night
merge with the background, darker than before.

Across the Square alumni celebrate,
then leave. I need more time to concentrate
alone, to seek what Bundy's not quite shown:
enlightenment. I probe a vast unknown.

TIME

i.m. Alice Maud Gray, 1890-1970

Often she calls us back to her
time, ten shillings a week and all
the fresh air of a sooty Hull street,
guarding herself against neighbours,
two bricks in her half-starved grate;
time fear changed its name
from Zeppelin to Relief Office,
her sewing machine indispensable
luxury gone for a child's new shoes;
time of her once higher standing
headstrong on an unglued wooden chair
stippling the stairway walls two-tone
distemper, old gold going modern;
time humming-happy crotcheting
the milk-white woollen poodle
to dress her bottle of cologne
with love she handed down;

time and time again a trim size ten,
vulnerable, tough as a hill-bred cob,
sniffing in rain and wind,
tongue sharp as her brain;
time with her at our table
where again today she sits in
on talk from Rawcliffe Grove
to East Mount Avenue, how
we'd walk her to the bus for home,
the mystery of the dark
Italian eyes her secret
kept beyond our lost goodbyes.

LIGHTS OUT

i.m. Vernon Scannell

A friend's gift of your book springs this response
which must be brief because it's getting late,
as I'll be soon and, sadly, you are now.
Dear Vernon, your *Last Post* reminds me, once,
at Lumb Bank circa nineteen-eightyeight
we met, when I had hopes you'd teach me how
to fine a poem from a grain of sand.
It doesn't work that way, I should have known
poetic art's not like a tool for hire.
Instead, you showed how best to play the hand
we're dealt in someone else's lines, where tone
and texture help a poem's tempo fire
imagination, captivate the mind.

Maestro, these poems bring to me a kind
of voice-mail sent from Coldenside again
where you declined to trumpet rhymes of yours
and selflessly espoused a nobler cause
re-living Hardy's 'During Wind and Rain',
but while I hear his rose "ript from the wall",
these pages say you haven't died at all
and, worlds away from hills of Heptonstall,
your voice rings clear, beyond the bugle's call.

THE FERTILE YEAR

Don't let them kid you being old's all sad,
nine weepy apertures, rheumatic pains –
they'll come of course but, till they do, be glad
for one who's found senility brings gains.

The writer's trough cuts deep and leaves behind
its threat of more, though, buoyed by caring friends,
can be survived; one surfaces to find
that paucities, like plethoras, have ends.

Blank days and workbooks, as they fill with love
and words of love become the panacea
long sought; a recharged pen begins to move
inquisitive along the fertile year,
age peels away, reveals a young man's brain
and maybe, on the page, a poem again.

LOOK, TWICE

Look at this frail old man and see
his rheumy eyes and pearl-hung nose,
the hands that shake incessantly;
look twice, more searchingly, and know
the chorister inside who sang
bel canto eighty years ago.
His *rallentando* won't take long
now, time's rip tide is far too strong
for both the singer and his song.

Look at this racked old woman, how
her ankles swell like gourds, her back
is arched, she can't stand upright now;
look twice and see again the fine
figura still inside, the girl
lit upstage from the chorus line.
Who knows if hell or heaven calls
the belle who thrilled the music halls –
or nothingness? The curtain falls.

AFTER OUR DIAMOND

December; scanning last year's list
of Christmas cards received – and missed,
we pause a while, reflect, and bless
Nye Bevan, for the NHS
and all the drugs that keep us here
or help to do so every year –
or have done, up to now.

It's not those cards that fail to come
concern us most, but always some
more pitiful, which newly bear
one partner's name alone. Here's where
we picture friends who'll feel the same
obliterating either name
of ours, not far from now.

LIGHT

after Frances Bellerby

When the sun bleeds over the edge
of the world one last time
for me – or for you – may our pledge
have been kept: that our home

should spell *love;* that we both understand
and forgive, each the friend
to warm the other's hand.
Shine, Dear Heart, to the end.

GOING OFF PISTE

It'll snow-blind 'em, cause 'em to blink
when I throw off the purple and red
and, with ever more brandy to drink,
I go stoned on wild SKI trips instead.

NOTES

HEINZ GROPSMEYER (page 7)
Wehrmacht: German Armed Forces.
Kölnischwasser: eau de Cologne; Cologne water.
Rotbart: Redbeard; a brand of razor blade.
Horst Wessel: a young German dissenter; a marching song.
*Gott: GOTT MIT UNS;*German army belt buckle motto.
Abschied: farewell; parting.
mezzogiorno: midday; synonym for the Italian impoverished
south.

TUTORIAL (page 58)
The tune: *When I Grow Too Old To Dream.*

SOLSTICE (page 68)
E.D. Suffered *lupus erythematosus.*

EX LIBRIS (page 72)
up the blue: in the desert (WWII)
soyas: sausage substitutes.
'V's: free-issue cigarettes.

ALL DOWN THE AVENUE (page 80)
Cartref: home.
Mamgu: Grandma.

ONLY CONNECT (page 82)
Edgar Bundy's *The Night School*, (1892), Ferens Art Gallery,
Hull.
R.H. Tawney's *An Experiment In Democratic Education*, (1914),
Political Quarterly.
'Only connect the prose and the passion, and both will be
exalted, and human love will be seen at its highest.' – E.M.
Forster, *Howards End.*

BOLT FOR FREEDOM (page 91)
The poet puppeteers:-
Dylan Thomas – 'Do not go gentle into that good night,'
Stevie Smith – 'Not waving, but drowning'

Wm. Wordsworth – Sonnet composed upon Westminster Bridge.
W.B. Yeats – 'The Lake Isle of Innisfree'
John Betjeman – 'Slough'
Tony Harrison – ' *v* '
Fiona Pitt-Kethley – 'Sky Ray Lolly'
Wendy Cope – 'Making Cocoa For Kingsley Amis'
Matt Simpson – 'Conscience on Mill Road'
Philip Larkin – 'Mr. Bleaney'
John Masefield – 'Cargoes'

RECAPTURE (page 92)
The captors:-
Edward Thomas – 'Liberty'
T.S. Eliot – 'La Figlia che Piange'
William Carlos Williams – 'The Red Wheelbarrow'
T.S. Eliot – 'The Waste Land'

BREWER (page 110)
Brewer: The Dictionary of Phrase and Fable compiled by The
Rev. E. Cobham Brewer, LLD., first published in 1870.

When the malt begins to get aboon the meal: when the drink
begins to talk. Sir Walter Scott, Old Mortality, ch 4.

Skalds of Scandinavia: poets, singers; scala: to sing.
Minnesingers of the Holy (German) Empire: Love-singers,
poets.

poet of the poor: Rev. George Crabbe (1754-1834)

the uncrowned prince: on his monument in Westminster Abbey,
Edmund Spenser (1553-1598) is called Prince of Poets.

the poetry of Persian, Arabic: Adam and Eve are said to have
spoken Persian, the most poetic of all languages, while the
serpent that seduced Eve spoke Arabic, the most persuasive
language in the world.

Characteristics of European languages
    L'Italien se parle aux dames.
    Le Francais se parle aux hommes.
    L'Anglais se parle aux oiseaux.
    L'Allemand se parle aux chevaux.
    L'espagnol se parle à Dieux.

Drunk as Chloe: Chloe, or Cloe (2 syl), is the cobbler's wife of Linden Grove, to whom Prior, the poet, was attached; she was notorious for her drinking.

DISPLACED PERSONS (page 113)
Naafi: Navy, Army & Air Force Insitute.
Amgot: Allied Military Government.
Abca: Army Bureau of Current Affairs.

KINDERWELT (page 131)
s*timmt: stimmen;* to agree/be correct.

BEHIND THE LINES (page 142)
Ausweis: identity card.
Geheimestaatspolizei: Gestapo; secret state police.
sotto voce: in an undertone.
'Johnny-get-your-gun' was a WWII mnemonic used in the training of soldiers to fire a Bren gun in bursts of five rounds, the easier to know when the magazine should be renewed.

FORLIMPÓPOLI (page 161)
non ti scordar di me: forget-me-not.
Tedeschi: Germans.
Grazie a Dio: thanks be to God.

LA GIOIOSA (page 162)
Buona Sera: Good Evening.

GOING OFF PISTE (page 170)
SKI: Spending the Kids' Inheritance.